# That They May . . .
# Train the
# Young Women

by

Ruth Thompson

ISBN 1-58427-049-7

Guardian of Truth Foundation
P.O. Box 9670
Bowling Green, Kentucky 42102

# Table of Contents

# Dedication

*I am dedicating this book to my husband,
Floyd Thompson, without whose encouragement
and help the work could not have been written.
Throughout more than forty-eight years of marriage,
his strength has been there to sustain me.
In appreciation for this encouragement,
these words are written.*

Ruth Thompson

*First Printing: 1980
Second Printing: 1980
Third Printing: 1984
Fourth Printing: 1995
Fifth Printing: 2004*

# Foreword

Since World War II every facet of American life has undergone tremendous change. Morals have plummeted to an alarming depth, which has left the home tottering on the brink of chaos. Young and old are being bombarded on every hand with salacious literature, entertainment and false teaching, all destructive of that which is godly and God-like. Even religious writings are influenced by the social philosophy of the day.

In the midst of such an atmosphere, this book by Mrs. Ruth Thompson will be welcomed by pious parents and faithful teachers who are looking for an aid in directing the lives of young women and girls. The book will come as a breath of fresh air in the midst of satanic pollution. In this series of lessons the author has made a worthwhile and worthy contribution to the instruction of young women by older women, as ordained by God.

The lessons are well arranged and organized, following the pattern set forth by the Holy Spirit in Paul's letter to Titus. This makes for ease in teaching and learning. They are interspersed with numerous Bible quotations, which enforce each point made. The lessons deal with vital areas in the character of young women, setting forth divine principles that go to make a wife and mother pleasing to God, thus laying the foundation for a happy home. If anything is to be salvaged from the wreck of our social system today, the older women *must* accept the role and responsibility toward young women that God has laid upon them.

Mrs. Thompson is eminently qualified to write such a series of lessons. For over forty years she has been the faithful wife and helpmate of an outstanding preacher and teacher of the word of God. For many of those years she has been a teacher of young women. She has known from necessity what it is to be frugal in life, to work at times that her husband

1

might devote his time to study and preaching, and at the same time to fill her role as a home-maker. She has drunk deeply from the fountain of truth, imbibing its spirit. Therefore she draws from a reservoir of experience and a life of Bible study. She herself is a living example of God's "worthy woman" of Proverbs 31.

Both pleasure and profit have been derived from reading the manuscript before its publication. It is a pleasure to recommend the book and to wish for it a wide circulation and intensive use. The homes of young Christians must be saved from Satan's destruction, and this can be done only by adherence to God's way as revealed in His book. God has chosen teaching of truth and its application in life as the means of building character and finding true happiness. Mrs. Thompson has stressed this throughout. The book is commended whole-heartedly.

In the long ago an un-named psalmist asked and answered the following question,

> "Wherewith shall a young man (or woman) cleanse his (or her) way? By taking heed thereto according to thy word" (Psalm 119:9).

Homer Hailey
Tucson, Arizona

# Preface

Several years ago, having been asked by the elders of my home congregation to prepare and teach a series of lessons for young women, the idea for this work was formulated. My co-teacher and helper in this series was a fellow-member of this same congregation, and together Cora Mae Arnold and I worked out the outline for the first classes. It was evident from the first that Titus 2:3-5 should be used as a basis for these studies. This scripture states: "That aged women likewise be reverent in demeanor, not slanderers nor enslaved to much wine; teachers of that which is good, *that they may train the young women* to (1) love their husbands, (2) to love their children, (3) to be sober-minded, (4) chaste, (5) workers at home, (6) kind, (7) being in subjection to their own husbands, that the word of God be not blasphemed."

Using this verse as a basis, the chapters (seven of them) were outlined as listed above. It is apparent that every phase of the work and duties of women is incorporated in these verses. Each chapter has been divided into several lessons, fifteen in all. Other scriptures have been used which relate to various phases of women's responsibilities, but this one text is full and complete.

Since the first class was begun and concluded, we have taught the same outline to other age groups, making revisions and expanding it as we deemed wise. Class ages have ranged from Senior High School to ladies in their sixties. All have received it well.

Because of the need today, just as in Paul's day on the island of Crete, I have been asked by several to put these lessons into book form for distribution to individuals or groups for study and class work. After serious consideration I have decided to go ahead with publication of this work. I realize that many others have set forth these same principles, that they have worthy works. However, it may be that I can bring

3

to light some truth that others may not have, or that I may present it in a way that some individual may be reached.

We are convinced that if the principles set forth herein are followed, they will produce within the lives of women the kind of godliness our Father wants for his children. We believe the world is in need of this training, that all people would be happier and better if the training were followed. Notice that the word "training" carries with it a deeper meaning than mere teaching. Training requires acceptation first, then practical application. God has always wanted only those things that are "good" for his children, and He has explicitly spelled out his rules for "goodness."

It is with mixed feelings that I undertake this work. However, I have the backing of a good husband, the encouragement of good elders, and the help and understanding of marvelous friends. Opposed to this encouragement is my own feeling of inadequacy. Nevertheless I submit these lessons to you and wish for you the success in your teaching program, and your own personal application, that such lessons merit.

All scriptures used herein are from the American Standard Version.

Ruth Thompson
Santa Ana, California

# Lesson 1

## That They May...
## "Train the Young Women"

**Introduction:**

How beautiful is youth! What a wonderful time of one's life! Everything that is fresh, new, and good is yours to enjoy. But youth is also the time to train for maturity and eternity. The way in which one's life is molded during youth will determine in a large way how you will conduct the balance of your life, and eventually, how you will spend eternity.

Then what does one want from life? Happiness? Of course, and one has a right to it. Everything good? Certainly every right-thinking person wants for herself the good things. The verse of scripture, the basis for our studies, exhorts the aged women to teach that which is good. One can have goodness; one can have happiness, too. We hope to impress on your minds during this study that the two goals, goodness and happiness, can both be achieved, and that they are compatible.

The verses of scripture that form the foundation for this series of lessons is found in Titus 2:3-5 and reads: "That aged women likewise be reverent in demeanor, not slanderers nor enslaved to much wine; teachers of that which is good, that they may train the young women to love their husbands, to love their children, to be soberminded, chaste, workers at home, kind, being in subjection to their own husbands, that the word of God be not blasphemed."

I want every person in this study to memorize the above

passage. It will be used over and over again in this work. Paul, an apostle of Christ, and an inspired writer, wrote this short letter to Titus. Paul had left Titus on the island of Crete. Moving on elsewhere, he had written back to this fine young worker, instructing him in carrying out God's will in the selection of elders and deacons, and other phases of organization. The background from which most of these Cretans came was one of idolatry. They sorely needed teaching on the relationships found in these verses. Women needed to know *how* to love their husbands, their children. They needed to know *how* to be in subjection, to be sober-minded, chaste, kind, workers at home. In the centuries following this writing, women, being influenced by the teaching in the scriptures, have come to know God's will. But now we come to another age, our own age, in which once again we are faced with the fact that mothers do not teach their daughters, old women do not teach young women these very principles. Once again we need to stress God's teaching on these things. Various women's organizations, including the Women's Liberation Movement have moved so fast and so powerfully that many false ideas of women's "rights" have evolved. These ideas have been received with tremendous success, even pervading the thinking of women in the church who should know better. Because of these false ideas, women of this age need this instruction.

That this period of life is a training ground for maturity is aptly told in this little story:

"Who made you?" the teacher asked a boy in his class.

"God made me," the boy replied quickly, "but I'm not finished yet!"

How vividly that answer presents the situation! God made me and placed me in the world. He continues to guide me, helping me through His word. But he depends upon me, too. He expects my cooperation in doing all I can to make myself "perfect," "mature," the "full-grown" individual he would have me to be. "My little children, of whom I am again in travail *until Christ be formed in you*" (Galatians 4:19). You have some growing up to do. No, "I am not finished yet." In this class, in these studies, we hope to be influential in turning out a more mature product who understands her role in this world.

Longfellow vividly described the beauty of youth when he wrote:

"How beautiful is youth! how bright it gleams
With its illusions, aspirations, dreams!
Book of Beginnings, story without End,
Each maid a heroine, and each man a friend!"

And still another said: "In Youth we learn; in Age we understand."

Knowing that you want and deserve these good things, let us study the meaning of the word "good" defined in the following:

- "God saw the light, that it was *good*" (Genesis 1:4) [Pleasing to God]
- "That thou mayest have *good* success" (Joshua 1:7) [To prosper]
- "*Good* in the sight of all the people" (1 Sam. 18:5) [Acceptable]
- "The *good* of his people" (Esther 10:3) [Wealth, benefit]
- "Turn away from evil, and do *good*"(1 Peter 3:11) [Righteousness]

Putting these definitions together we understand that God expects older women to teach that which is *pleasing to God,* that which will cause *your soul to prosper,* that which is *acceptable in the sight of God,* that which will *benefit* you in this life and that which is to come, and lastly, teachers of that which is *good.* What a tremendous challenge lies before us! This paragraph could be summed up in the statement that we hope to be teachers of God's word, since it is through this word that we know what He expects of us in the realm of goodness.

All of God's commandments are righteousness, and righteousness is that which is good. A teacher should train young women to do what God wants them to do, never teach them evil, nor anything slightly contrary to God's word. If the older women keep this in mind, then no matter what the subject on which you are teaching, it can do nothing but good

7

for the young women.

**Our Goal:** The aim of these lessons is to direct young women for their future roles, and eventually for eternity. When this particular study is concluded we hope that purpose will have been accomplished. It is a study that needs to be taught regularly, from time to time. Within a few months, another similar study could be made with another age group. There will always be the need for repetition of these principles, just as there is a need for teaching on other phases of our moral responsibilities. I could suggest a yearly, and once every two years study. I think it would be profitable for every church.

In our study we want to:

1. Stay with the outline. We will bear in mind that you will have areas within this outline in which you will be especially interested. We want to discuss those things with you.

2. Learn more of God's will as it relates to these topics.

3. Stress the point that my opinion will not be the basis of the study, though there may be times that both the student and the teacher may express an opinion. When I do, I will let you know that it is but my opinion.

4. Insist that the student also ask questions, express opinions, feel free to be a part of class discussions on all subjects, remembering that the direction of this study is scripture-bound, not opinion-bound.

5. Follow the outline, at least loosely. Glance over your outline and see if the question you want to ask is included elsewhere in our study. If so, it would be better to wait until we get to that particular part. This will make for a more cohesive study.

### You Are Accountable

Before getting into the study proper we want to stress the fact that every person is accountable to God for his actions. Some people have a feeling that they have a moral right to disregard God's commands. You do have the will, the ability, to disregard his commands, since God made you a free moral agent. But you do not have the *moral right* to do so. God, our Creator, has set the standard for what is right. Paul, quoting from Isaiah, said, "For it is written, As I live, saith the Lord, to me every knee shall bow, and every tongue shall confess to God. So then each one of us shall give account of himself to God" (Romans 14:11,12; Isaiah 45:23). Our acceptance or rejection of this principle does not void it. God's law stands for every one of his creatures, whether they accept it or not. Each is accountable to him.

We stand separated from God until we repent of our sins and are forgiven. Though we are not born in sin, we do sin and separate ourselves from God. Isaiah said, "But your iniquities have separated between you and your God, and your sins have hid his face from you, so that He will not hear" (Isaiah 59:2). Young people, you have the obligation to set an example before the world. Paul said to Timothy, "Let no man despise thy youth; but be thou an example to them that believe; in word, in manner of life, in love, in faith, in purity" (1 Timothy 4:12).

God, who knows our frame and knows what is good for us, said, "It is good for a man that he bear the yoke in his youth" (Lamentations 3:27).

If we bear the yoke in our youth our soul will prosper, we will be acceptable in the sight of God, it will bring us a wealth of happiness, it will benefit us, it will give us everything that is the opposite of evil. What a challenge! What a reward!

## Learn To Accept Yourself

One of the hardest things psychiatrists confront in dealing with people is to get them to accept themselves as they are. This can be a problem with women today, especially in these modern times. Women's organizations have stressed the idea that women are not getting what they are entitled to receive. They try to educate women in the belief that women and men are equal. In some respects this is true. Women are as good, they are as bright, they are as much respected in the sight of God as men. But to say that men and women are "the same" just is not true. They are two separate beings. They are given different roles to perform by God. The sooner we recognize this basic fact, the sooner we can undo some of the erroneous ideas put forth by the modern school of thought.

Our first need therefore is to emphasize the fact that you

9

are a woman. If you have not already accepted this fact of life, we need to teach you in what respects you are different. You are a woman! I once heard someone say that she wished she had been a bird! A very fanciful wish indeed! She could just flit from limb to limb, singing all day long! This is a wish that would be impossible to achieve, and one that we recognize as being mere fancy. Likewise I have heard many girls say they wish they had been born men. This is just as fanciful as the first. You can no more be a man than you can be a bird (notwithstanding some recent experiments in this realm). Therefore the primary goal in this class is to establish the fact that you are what you are, that nothing can change it. The sooner you accept your role in the creation of God, the sooner you can begin to make it what God expects of you, that of a godly woman, a creation of His.

"And now, Israel, what doth Jehovah thy God require of thee, but to fear Jehovah thy God, to walk in all his ways, and to love Him and to serve Jehovah thy God with all thy heart and with all thy soul, to keep the commandments of Jehovah, and his statutes, which I command thee this day *for thy good?*" (Deuteronomy 10:12-13).

"For He knoweth our frame; he remembereth that we are dust" (Psalms 103:14).

God wants only what is *good* for us, and He *knows* our frame. He knows, sees, and understands us from the inside out. He knows us so much better than we know ourselves. He knows what will make us happy. I will be referring to these two verses of scripture often throughout this study. I cannot impress too deeply on your minds the forcefulness of these verses in our study. Whatever Jehovah teaches in His word about women's role in this life, have confidence in the fact that He *knows* us and wants what is best and *good* for us.

### Dare To Be Different

I hear a lot these days about being one's self, "doing your own thing." I hear much against being a conformist, but I do not see a great deal of it being practiced. Just as in the past, just as it will be in the future, present-day young people want to do what the majority of their peer group does. This in itself is not bad. Everyone wants to "belong." But

10

when the group goes contrary to what God teaches then a Christian, whether young or old, must develop the courage to say no, to be different. Remember, the majority is usually wrong. God has said, "Thou shalt not follow a multitude to do evil . . ." (Exodus 23:2). Rather than following a multitude to do evil, God teaches us ". . . to the intent that, denying ungodliness and worldly lusts, we should live soberly and righteously and godly in this present world" (Titus 2:12).

Some temptations are prevalent with youth that the older folk do not have, but one does not have to succumb to these temptations. God tells us not to: "But flee youthful lusts, and follow after righteousness, faith, love, peace, with them that call on the Lord out of a pure heart" (2 Timothy 2:22).

## Questions On
## LESSON NO. 1

1. Which verse of scripture forms the basis for the study of this series of lessons? Have you memorized it?

2. What do we want and what should we expect to gain out of life?

3. Our lives are a training ground for what important thing?

4. Give the Bible definition of the word "good." Give scriptural definitions and citations.

5. What is the goal in this class?

6. Name the hardest thing we have to learn about accepting ourselves, and why is it necessary that we do?

7. Did God ever give us a commandment that was not good for us? If so, cite scripture.

8. Does God know His creation? Where does the Bible so state?

9. Name some of the things in this study with which we shall be dealing.

10. Are all people accountable to God? Support your answer.

11. Should a person wait until old age to do God's commandments? Cite scripture.

12. Do you have a longing to be "part of the crowd?" Is that wrong?

13. Under what circumstances should one not follow the crowd? Cite scripture.

# Chapter One      Lesson 2

# "To Love
# Their Husbands"

Some of you who are studying this lesson already have husbands; others hope soon to have them; and of the rest, at least most of you hope someday to have husbands. So, in whichever class you find yourself, this lesson is applicable to you. We older women, with years of wifehood behind us, would have profited by studying just such lessons in our youth. There are many fundamental facts about men and their relationships with women, that need to be fully understood. Until you do understand them, you are not ready for marriage. If you are already married, you can profit by the study, and perhaps better the relationship between the two of you.

Fortunately most of you have been brought up by parents who are christians, and who understand your need for such training. That is a great advantage in our society. Many young women in the world receive no such training, either by parents or teachers. They enter into matrimony with no idea of how to make a home, or what it means to love their husbands in the true sense of the word "love." If perchance their marriage does work, they are fortunate. But the high divorce rate in this country tells the sad story of the ignorance on the part of both parties. Most marriages fail, ending up in the divorce court. The couple has little conception of fault or how to avoid it. Some few of them hang on, but live in a state of unhappiness their entire married lives. The situation on the pagan island of Crete was similar to the world of today. Their ignorance of God's will in such matters prompted Paul to instruct Titus in informing them.

God did not intend that marriage should be an unhappy state. Marriage should be the most sacred and closest union in which a man and woman can enter, resulting in complete happiness for both.

Marriage is ordained of God. The role of wife was the first one given woman, Eve. God gave her in marriage, intending that the relationship last for life. Some Pharisees came to Jesus, trying him, and saying "Is it lawful for a man to put away his wife for every cause? And He answered and said, Have ye not read, that he who made them from the beginning made them male and female, and said, For this cause shall a man leave his father and mother and shall cleave to his wife; and the two shall become one flesh? What therefore God hath joined together, let not man put asunder. They say unto him, Why then did Moses command to give a bill of divorcement, and to put her away? He saith unto them, Moses *for your hardness of heart* suffered you to put away your wives: but from the beginning it hath not been so" (Matthew 19:3-8). Verse 8 stresses that God intended this marriage to last a lifetime. Though man may break this relationship, as he did in Moses' day, it is not pleasing to God.

Having established that marriage is good, let us further study God's word on passages that teach us the order, the arrangement, the plan God made for man and woman. Since we have accepted the fact that we are women, that we should not try to change that arrangement, so should women accept the fact that God made a proper realm of activity for each of his creation.

Here is the God-ordained order: "But I would have you know that the head of every man is Christ" (1 Corinthians 11:3). We do not have any quarrel with that arrangement, do we? Any right-thinking person accepts Christ as his head joyfully, knowing it is God's arrangement. And now: "And the head of Christ is God." We know and accept God as the Father over his creation and Christ as his Son under Him. To

14

substantiate this idea, Paul tells us, "When all things shall have been subjected unto him, then shall the Son also himself be subjected to him who did subject all things unto him, that God may be all in all" (1 Corinthians 15:28). We understand this to teach that God has given authority to Christ now to reign over His kingdom, but that when he brings this world to an end Christ will deliver the kingdom back to the Father and be in subjection to Him, as before. This arrangement does not cause us any problems, does it?

But now I wish you to listen to the next part of this scripture: "And the head of the woman is the man." Modern society, influenced by the women's liberation movement and other related organizations, rejects this teaching. We should accept it. If we do not we simply assert our opinion over God's expressed order. Our plea with you is to accept it. Remember — "God knows our frame" and knows the best arrangement.

God's arrangement originated with the first couple, Adam and Eve. God made Adam of the dust of the earth, and breathed into his nostrils the breath of life. Adam became a living soul, made in the image of God. Then God saw that it was not good that man should live alone, and said, "I will make him a help meet (good) for him" (Genesis 2:18). Jehovah caused a deep sleep to fall upon Adam, took from his body a rib and from it created woman. He brought her to Adam who said, "This is now bone of my bones, and flesh of my flesh: she shall be called Woman, because she was taken out of man. Therefore shall a man leave his father and his mother, and shall cleave unto his wife: and they shall be one flesh" (Genesis 2:23,24).

It is quite apparent that God made a perfect relationship. Adam and Eve complemented each other perfectly. Each has his own realm of operation, but each is dependent upon the other for companionship, for sustenance and for love. A perfect union! I think of the union of two people as a "partnership" in which each partner has an equal interest in the union. They share the good times, but also the bad. They each put into that partnership the very best planning they can, and each is equally interested in seeing that it "goes."

Peter speaks of marriage as a union of two people who are "joint heirs" of the grace of life. It is not an arrangement by which one profits, and the other does not. Both profit, if the marriage is properly conducted as God would have it. This is what God wants for his creation in the marriage relationship, and we can be happy with this arrangement.

Sin entered into the world when Eve yielded to the temptation of the devil and ate of the forbidden fruit. When she gave to Adam, and he did also eat, God said to the man, "Because thou hast hearkened unto the voice of thy wife, and hast eaten of the tree, of which I commanded thee, saying, Thou shalt not eat of it; cursed is the ground for thy sake: in toil shalt thou eat of it all the days of thy life: thorns also and thistles shall it bring forth to thee: and thou shalt eat the herb of the field; in the sweat of thy face shalt thou eat bread till thou return to the ground: for out of it wast thou taken; for dust thou art and unto dust shalt thou return" (Genesis 3:17-19).

Then God spoke to Eve, saying, "I will greatly multiply thy pain and thy conception; in pain shalt thou bring forth children, and thy desire shall be to thy husband, and *he shall rule over thee"* (Genesis 3:16).

Just as surely as man has to work to make a living, just that surely woman's desire shall be to her husband and he shall rule over her. God's promises do not fail.

Many are the admonitions in the New Testament concerning woman's being in subjection to her husband. Let's notice a few:

• "But I permit not a woman to teach, nor to have dominion over a man, but to be in quietness. For Adam was first formed, then Eve" (1 Timothy 2:12,13).

• "Wives, be in subjection unto your own husbands, as unto the Lord. For the husband is the head of the wife, as Christ also is the head of the church . . ." (Ephesians 5:22,23).

• "In like manner, ye wives, be in subjection to your own husbands" (1 Peter 3:1). And in Verse 5, ". . . being in subjection to their own husbands."

This passage discusses the example Sarah set in obeying her husband when Peter said, ". . . as Sarah obeyed Abraham,

16

calling him Lord, whose children ye now are, if ye do well, and are not put in fear by any terror" (1 Peter 3:6).

How did Sarah obey Abraham? There was a time in their lives when they were childless. Sarah was past the time of bearing children. But God came to them and promised them a child. More than just a child, a child of promise through whom the Messiah was to be born. But they could not understand all that God had in mind for them. As time passed and Sarah still had not conceived, she devised her own plan for bringing about God's promise. This philosophy gets into the thinking of so many people today. Not satisfied with God's arrangement for his children, not happy with his time-clock, they try to devise human arrangements for carrying out his word. God will not allow such arrangements, either then or now. But Sarah worked out a scheme, proposed it to Abraham, and together they carried it out. The proposal was that they take Sarah's handmaid, Hagar, and have a child by her. The child born of this union was called Ishmael. God visited them again and let them know that this was not his planning. Eventually Sarah got the idea that God was ruling in their lives, and that His planning would prevail. Then she became the obedient wife that she should have been. She waited for God's plan to materialize, became the mother of Isaac, the child of promise, and the mother of a great nation, the Israelites. Through this lineage, she also became the mother of a spiritual nation, God's church. Then, but not till then, could it truly be said of her, "For after this manner aforetime the holy women also, who hoped in God, adorned themselves, *being in subjection to their own husbands;* as Sarah obeyed Abraham, calling him lord; whose children ye now are, if ye do well, and are not put in fear by any terror" (1 Peter 3:5,6).

## Questions On
## LESSON NO. 2

1. Is it natural for a woman to want a husband and a home?

2. Why is it necessary to teach on this subject?

3. Can we all profit by such a study? How?

4. Did God intend marriage to last? How do you know?

5. Who ordained marriage in the first place? Give scripture.

6. What was the order, or the arrangement, of God's creation?

7. Should we doubt the wisdom of God's arrangement? Should we seek to change it?

8. What is the current trend in the world today concerning God's arrangement? How does this violate God's word?

9. When and how did man first violate God's perfect plan for him?

10. What was God's punishment for this sin? How do we know he was displeased?

11. What is God's plan in woman's relationship to man?

12. What does 1 Timothy 2:13 say regarding woman's place in God's scheme?

13. Quote Ephesians 5:22,23. Give the meaning of this passage.

14. What does Peter say about woman's relationship to man?

15. Tell the story of Sarah's plan to give Abraham a child. Why was this not acceptable? What was the outcome?

# "To Love Their Husbands"

### Understanding Men

Men have certain God-given qualities that constitute their make-up. Unless we know what these qualities are, and learn how to deal with them we can never understand nor appreciate the man we have chosen to be our life companion. His needs may vary from yours, but they need to be fulfilled, and you are the one to fulfill them.

Let us examine some of these needs:

*1. Appreciate the Good Qualities He Does Have.*

Something about him attracted you to him in the first place. Often a woman will set about to remake a man into her own idea of what a husband or a man should be. This is a mistake. He is entitled to keep whatever traits he has. You must acknowledge his right to be accepted for himself just as you hope he will accept you as you are. If changes come (and they will) let them come from within him. Be happy! Be in a good state of mind in accepting him! Do not have a martyred or a self-righteous attitude. And above all, do not use other men as shining examples. This goes over like a lead balloon. Look to his better side, and dwell on those qualities.

*2. Express Your Appreciation for the Traits You Admire.*

He *wants* you to admire his manly qualities. Watch the small boy at play with girls. He will exert himself to the utmost to impress them with what he can do, how much he

20

can lift, and how big and strong he is. Grown men do the same thing, though generally speaking they are less obvious. Men have qualities that women do not have. They can drive a nail, fix a car, mend a door, and balance a checkbook. Perhaps you can do these things, too, but it is a blow to his pride to know you think you can do them better than he. Allow him the privilege of being better than you in these manly traits.

Here are some of the ways you can express your appreciation for his talents:

*a. Let your mind dwell on his manliness.* Women are prone to discount what their husbands can do. This is especially true as time goes by. We develop a tendency to take him for granted, which is a big mistake. Never take him for granted. Develop the attitude toward him that he is something special that has come into your life, and that you are *aware* of his qualities and appreciative of them. If you *think* about his manliness enough you soon will come to appreciate him for what he is. It will become a vital part of your lives, and of your role as wives.

*b. Really look at him.* Take time to study his good points; elaborate on them. The tendency is to overlook his good points and elaborate on weak points. Those traits that are not particularly appealing will stand out like a sore thumb. This is not the way to develop a good and lasting relationship in marriage. As a matter of fact this is not the way to develop a good relationship with anyone. This kind of person becomes more and more critical, less and less charitable to weaknesses in others, at the same time thinking of yourself as the model of perfection. If you will take the time to observe people you cannot fail to see good points in them. This is especially true of a marriage relationship. After a while you will be surprised to find he has so many good traits.

This point reminds me of the story of an old woman who was renowned for never saying anything critical of anyone. A few people trying to trick her into saying something bad about someone, asked, "Granny, what do you think of the devil?" She replied, "Well, if we all worked as hard as he does, we'd get more done."

21

*c. When he talks, listen.* Wives tend to disregard what their husbands say. You can observe this in a roomful of older people. A woman may pay close attention to what everyone else says, but just let her husband speak up and she doesn't hear a word he says.

When your husband comes in from work the thing he wants most is a quiet, well-ordered household, where he can talk off the frustrations of the day and have someone who will listen and sympathize with his problems. Develop the trait of listening when he speaks. Do not try to anticipate him, and do not interrupt his story. Do not beat him to the punch line if he is telling a good story in company. Just wait until he says what is on his mind. A good listener is the best therapy anyone can have. He does not really want you to solve his problem for him. A suggestion in good taste might be in order, but it is better if he solves his own. Your listening sympathetically to his problem will work wonders for him.

*d. Be lavish with praise.* Never be selfish or stingy about telling him how much you appreciate his efforts. If you are sincere (and hopefully you will be) he will know it and appreciate your praise. If you cannot be sincere in your praise of something he has done, it is better to be quiet. He would soon know how insincere you were and would no longer trust your "flattery," as that is what it would be.

*e. Pinpoint compliments.* If he has accomplished something, no matter how small or how large, point out that specific thing and tell him how good you think he is in this accomplishment. Don't waste your time with praise like, "That was pretty good, all right." Say things more to the point, such as, "You know, I don't know of anyone that could have found the words that you did on that point. Your argument was to the point and could not have been better answered." Or, "You have a special knack for mechanics (painting, carpentering). Think of the money you saved by knowing how to fix it so well yourself."

*3. Do Not Humiliate Him.*

A man's pride is the backbone of his character. His need to retain that pride is very real. This is one of the areas that a wife can do the most damage, because pride is easily damaged.

She can contradict him before others, or in private. She can be indifferent to him. Because he is sensitive he suffers many problems. When you belittle him he builds up a wall of reserve against you. He will not tell you of his hopes, dreams and plans. Years of belittling him will cause him to keep these things to himself for fear of humiliation or indifference. It has a numbing effect on him. He may even resort to dishonesty rather than go through more humiliation from your ridicule. Did you ever wonder why your husband doesn't tell you about anything? Perhaps it is because you have been indifferent to his previous attempts, or that you made fun of his ideas. At least, take a long, hard look at yourself to see if you have been guilty of such a thing.

*4. Understand and Sympathize With His Needs.*

Making the living is the man's sphere. He worries about it; it becomes a constant, pressing problem with him. One day as my husband and I were riding he asked me, "Do you ever worry about having a job or whether or not we can make ends meet?" I told him it never crossed my mind. Then I asked him, "Do you?" He replied, "All the time. Not that I worry or am afraid of going hungry. But I know the responsibility to make a living is mine, and I am constantly concerned with how best to accomplish it."

Until the recent influx of women into the job market it was the men who died of heart attacks, brought on mainly by the tensions and pressures of making a living. Now, with women occupying the same areas, heart attacks are becoming more common with them also. Ulcers, nervous breakdowns, and related diseases are common to men because of these pressures. You can be a big help to your husband, and a real help meet (good) for him in this area by following these suggestions:

*a. Watching that budget.* You can do this in so many ways. Even in these days of inflated prices you can shop for and find bargains in the grocery and clothing stores. Keeping up with the Jones's is the most common fault with many wives. "Things" become so important in their lives that they fail to see what they are doing to their husbands. Their constant nagging for "things" gnaws at the heart of every husband, and keeps his nose to the grindstone. Overwork, moon-lighting, or any other way to make a little more to supply an ever-increasing demand will cause him to finally reach the end of his endurance. Either he ends up with a heart attack, an ulcer, a nervous breakdown or hypertension, or he simply walks out on the marriage. There are more "demands" than his abilities can provide. How nice it would be for him if, instead of badgering him with constant "wants," you would create within the home an atmosphere of love, good taste and pleasantness, regardless of your income. If you could provide a home where good food is served in pleasant surroundings, where he is met with a smile and pleasantries rather than pouting and nagging, he would be one of the happiest and most fortunate of men.

In accomplishing this aim, make out a good budget and stick to it. When buying food, watch for bargains. Find ways to S-T-R-E-T-C-H that dollar. In an article entitled "Home Management," the author lists twenty ways to stretch your dollar. I will mention only the headings, and you can do your own analysis:

(1) Wait for sales (2) Use coupons
(3) Shop by menu (4) Check all bills
(5) Re-use it (6) Buy in bulk
(7) Research major purchases(8) Save energy
(9) Use house brands (10) Do it yourself
(11) Bypass convenience foods(12)Shop prices
(13) Use cars economically (14) Fix it up
(15) Bargain over price (16) Barter (swap skills)
(17) Stick to your list (18) Use special fares
(19) Get help from friends (20) Give something you
made

[from *Courier,* February, 1979]

I can think of other suggestions. Do not throw good food away. Find ways to use it attractively and tastefully. Your clothing budget need not include all the latest styles. You do not have to dress like a fashion plate. Learn to sew. I am so glad to see the trend back to sewing. Many young girls sew now. It is a good thing to know, more especially when youngsters come along. Their clothing is often as high

24

as for adults.  Many precious dollars can be saved by doing it yourself.

When you are first married, just establishing your own home, and until finances permit, you can do without all the newest gadgets.  Sure, they make keeping house a little easier, but you can still wash dishes by hand.  Too many young married couples want to begin housekeeping with a large, four-bedroom home, all the built-ins, two or three television sets, stereo system, water beds, rumpus room, family room, fireplace, two cars, bicycles, motorcycles, a boat, a camper, a trailer, a mountain cabin and vacations every year to far-away places, trying at the same time to keep up with all the latest fashions and shows.  They think if they are not having or doing all these, they just simply are not living!  How sad!  Some people have been keeping house for fifty years and still do not have all those things, and never really expect to.  There is something else about that which may seem even stranger to you!  There comes a time when one knows that "things" are not that important.  Though you may be able to afford them now you really do not want them.  Does that sound strange?  It is not.  It is simply a basic fact of life.  Some fortunate people learn this early in life, and how good it is that they do.  They are way out ahead of those who have to learn it later, if at all.  Be appreciative of small things and learn to enjoy them.

*b. Quit expecting so much of your husband.*  This is another way in which we can give our husbands sympathetic understanding.  A great mistake wives often make is in meeting their husbands at the door with all the complaints of their day.  The moment they see them they unload every little thing that happened to them that day.  It is dumped in his lap the moment he comes in the door.  Put yourself in his place for just a moment!  He has had a very trying day at work.  Many problems have come up with which he has had to deal.  He is tired.  His one thought is what a relief it will be to get home, sit down in an easy chair, take off his shoes and let his mind go completely blank, a surcease from all the worries of his day.  But what happens?  The wife meets him and completely envelops him in the problems of her day.  Some of them may be petty, not worth bringing to him in the

25

first place. But even supposing a few of them are weighty problems that you feel need discussing and with which you have not been able to cope. At least give him a chance to relax and work off some of his own frustrations. By that time you will probably have forgotten some of your own. Then together you can have a relaxed atmosphere in which to discuss the big problems.

Think about *him* when you are contemplating making plans for the evening. Is it a good night for him? Is he tired? Are you demanding more of him than he is really able to give? Spend more time on creating and providing a restful atmosphere in which he can recuperate from the pressing duties of making a living for his family.

*c. Look like his wife, not his buddy.* I am not advocating "dressing" for dinner. But just check your appearance before his arrival. Present a neat, tidy and feminine appearance when he comes home from work. Let him know you love him and are glad he is home with you again after a long day away from you. Give him something to which he will be happy to come home. This is your God-given role. Have a happy home, leaning on the man for strength.

*d. Is he ever in a bad mood?* Make allowances for these times. You yourself sometimes are in a bad mood, so why would it be so strange for him? Perhaps things have happened to him at work that day, disturbing him no end. He has had no opportunity to "vent his pent-up emotions." When he comes into his home he may find that the ideal time to let off steam. He is not really taking it out on you; you were just there when he had his first chance to pop off. Be sweet, sympathetic and understanding, and it will soon pass. But if you make this the time for getting back at him, expressing all the pent-up dissatisfactions you have, then this can become the battleground for needless and unending quarreling and bickering.

*e. Complaining.* Some of his actions may "bug" you no end. Mistakes common to most of us, mistakes we make that can create big problems and reveal our lack of understanding are these:

- "You're late again!" Your mistake is in making a big

26

thing of it. I read recently about a young, wise woman who had prepared a special dinner for that first anniversary. He did not arrive at the appointed hour. Soon the phone rang. It was he, explaining that he was with a client showing a house, and would be late for dinner. She could have thought, "This is our first anniversary! He doesn't love me. He's ruined the whole evening!" But she didn't. She put the food in the warming oven, began reading the Bible, and when he came home an hour later she served the best meal possible in the best attitude she could muster. They had a quiet, beautiful evening, and it went off just as well as if he had appeared on time. No one was mad or hurt. Every moment was a precious one to store up in memory.

• "You spend more time with others than you do with me. You love your job more than your family!" How often has a man heard these purely imaginative complaints. It is probably true that he spends more time on the job than he does with you. But the reason is not that he loves his job more. The reason is that he cannot properly support his number one love, his family, without devoting more time to his job than he does to his family. That is his motive for working, if he is a right-thinking individual. Never try to allocate just how much time should be allotted to you, and how much to a job. Just know that if you are to be together at all a job demands a certain amount of his time.

• "You don't do anything to help out around the house." Maybe not. It is possible though that he does more than you realize. But honestly, now, just what *are* his household chores? I know men who are no good at all with a hammer, with a shovel, or with a lawnmower. It is even possible that their wives are better than they with these implements. That does not mean that he is neglectful. It simply means that he is better at some things than at others in which he has no particular interest. He probably is very good at his job, or at other things in which you have little interest. Again, if you do not feel that you should be doing these chores yourself, leave it up to him to see that they are done in the way that he deems best. If you *want* to do them, go ahead.

• "You do not manage money well." This is another

27

oft-made complaint with some wives. Some women think they are better money managers, and demand that their husbands hand over the paycheck the moment he brings it home. There may be rare instances in which this is necessary. Some men, realizing some weakness in themselves, have even asked their wives to do this, simply giving them spending money for the week. I think this is a very poor arrangement, and one that should be avoided at any cost, if possible. It should be used only as a last resort, and then at his suggestion. If you are the one who makes such an arrangement, you are away out of line. I suppose there is more bickering over money in most homes than over any other thing. This should never be. You should know what he can afford for you to spend on household necessities, then make it your business to stay within that figure. He should recognize that emergencies occur, that some latitude can be expected. Both of you should be generous but not extravagant in the handling of your funds.

## Questions On
## LESSON NO. 3

1. Is it true that men have certain God-given qualities? Do they vary from that of the women?

2. Why would it not be wise to try to re-make the man you intend to marry?

3. Discuss the ways in which you can accept him for what he is.

4. Talk about his need for your appreciation for his good traits.

5. List some of the ways in which you can teach yourself to admire the man you chose.

6. Are men sensitive to humiliation? In what ways can we harm them?

7. Why should you be concerned with being sympathetic and understanding?

8. Name some of his pressing responsibilities in the area of providing.

9. Talk about some of the ways we can relieve these worries.

10. Should a wife expect "things" in abundance in the early stages of a marriage? In any stage thereafter?

11. How should a wife greet her husband at the end of his work day?

12. Will you ever have to make allowances for his "bad behavior?" Why should we?

13. Tell me some of the complaints husbands often hear from their wives? Discuss.

# "To Love
# Their Husbands"

### Understanding Men

Thus far in this chapter, "To Love Their Husbands," we have studied in depth the ways in which we can learn to appreciate the good qualities that men have, expressing that appreciation, and being sympathetic with their needs, meanwhile doing nothing to humiliate nor degrade them. Now we are ready to study the values of *leadership*, and how we may be able to recognize and bring out in them the quality of the leadership they should have.

### I. LEADERSHIP AND RECOGNITION

The innate desire on the part of a man for leadership and recognition is inborn, a part of his male ego, his make-up. It is God-given and natural. A wife should never discourage her husband in his attempt to achieve a place in the world in which he operates, whether it be a business, a trade, a profession or a position. He takes great satisfaction in making progress, in achieving success in his chosen field. A great part of his satisfaction lies in the fact that *you* recognize him for what he can do. Do not forget this, and be rewarded for your perception by seeing that pleased gleam in his eyes.

In trying to achieve success, men sometimes meet with setbacks and failures. At times like these he needs sympathy, not criticism. You can be of great help to him if you understand that he is discouraged and needs you. There are many

31

ways in which the wife can be of real help at these discouraging times. A mistake at this point could be fatal to his success in life or to your marriage. Though you should not try to solve his problem for him, you might help by suggesting or stating an opinion, leaving it up to his best judgment to accept or reject. Try to be a good listener at these times in order to better understand his problems and deep feelings. Let him know of your concern and sympathy. Cause him to feel that you have an equal concern in what concerns him. Try to understand that he considers this problem a grave one, and do not minimize it. An off-hand remark such as, "Oh, that doesn't amount to anything," or, "Forget it," doesn't help his feelings nor the problem.

Also, he knows as well as you do that he has other blessings for which to be thankful. So don't rub that point, like rubbing salt into a wound. At this moment he is concerned with this one problem; and you should be, too.

Make him understand that your confidence in him is great. You know that he can work it out, so tell him so. Offer to do what he suggests as a means of working it out. In that way he will know he can count on your standing behind him, no matter what the cost.

Above all don't be a "gloomy-gus," and throw cold water on all his suggestions. Actions or words that say, "I knew you'd get us into something like this" would surely destroy his self-confidence and his will to try.

Your husband should have first priority in your life, even over:

*a. The Children:* As children come along many wives make the mistake of letting them absorb all their time. From the moment the first baby arrives she thinks of nothing but the comfort and well-being of that child. This is the time when the husband can begin to feel neglected, like an outsider in his own home. He tries to enter into the happy picture but he cannot get as close as he used to be. Something has gone out of the marriage, and that something was very precious. Once gone it will be hard to restore. The best thing to do is to remember that though children make many demands on the mother's time, that though they bring sweetness and light into your life, the husband is still there and needs you, too, as much as a child does. Resolve that you will make a time for him and you to be as close, and the relationship as sacred, as it was before. This can be a thing on which to work. There are many ways it can be done. You can include him in your plans for seeing to the baby, for asking him into the nursery, and for arranging your time so that when the baby is sleeping you have time to be alone with him.

How should the children expect to be treated concerning the things they want? I knew one young lady whose husband was even then on partial charity, who never failed to buy a toy off the rack at the grocery when she went shopping, simply because a two-year-old child asked for it. I saw that same child bring the toy home, play with it for five minutes, and discard it forever. Learn to say "no" to some of the things for which your child asks. It will do him good to learn that he cannot have everything he wants.

Even your interest and thought concerning the children can be detrimental to your husband. If every word of your conversation is dictated by your complete absorption in your child, it narrows your thinking too much, and makes of you a shriveled person. Some day that child will be gone, and you will be left without anything to talk about. Occasionally this very thing brings about a separation of married couples after the children leave home. They find themselves alone with a total stranger. Too much time was devoted to the children to the exclusion of a good rapport with each other.

*b. Where We Live:* What about the decision as to where you are going to live? In what city, what state, what house? Sometimes a mother will allow the children to make this decision; or the wife herself makes it on the basis of what the children like to do. This is not the primary motive for living at a certain address. The primary motive is whether it is in the best interest of the man's job, or his financial ability, or his own preference. Young lady, you should recognize this and be willing to go where he wants to go, live where he wants to live, let him be the one to decide where he wants to work, and the kind of work he wants to do. Until you learn this you have not *begun* to learn the role God has given to wives.

*c. How I Keep the House:* When I say that a woman can devote too much time to the art of homemaking it sounds as if I were contradicting myself. But I am not, and you will soon see my reasoning behind the statement. Though most men appreciate a clean house, good food, a warm atmosphere created by you in your home, they do not appreciate it to the exclusion of him and his interests. Nor to the exclusion of your good disposition. In reality homemaking *can* become an obsession, just like anything else. Above all do not let your homemaking interfere with his enjoyment of it. He provided the home for you, and we agree that you should be proud of it, making it as nice a home as your limited funds will permit. But let him feel at home in his own house. If he wants to sit on the edge of the bed to put on his shoes and socks, don't object. Just remember that he bought the mattress and that when this one goes it will be his money that provides another. Does he want to take off his shoes and put his feet up on the coffee table? Don't complain; be glad he wants to be there, to feel at home there. Are you so tired at the end of a long day of cleaning and cooking, scouring and scrubbing that you cannot enjoy his company? Just save a little of that energy for a good relationship with him. I remember early in my own marriage that my husband told me he would rather have me meet him at the door with a smile, glowing with happiness, than to have everything spic and span in the house and be met with frowns and grumpiness. From one who appreciates a well-organized home, that is a revealing statement, one that needs to be considered. This does not give you the license to "let things go." This phase of your work will be discussed at length in another lesson.

*d. Personal Appearance:* Spend enough time on your own personal appearance to present a neat and appealing front to the world. Slovenliness does not become anyone. Much time could be spent on cleanliness, and how God expects his children to be industrious and diligent in their entire life pattern. But personal appearance *to the exclusion* of having time for husband, children or home is pure folly. It is selfishness to the highest degree. Some things to remember about having more

34

time is simplicity of dress and grooming. You can be neat and clean, your hair can be attractive, if you practice simplicity in all your dress habits. Spending hours each week on elaborate hair-dos, thirty minutes or more each day putting on make-up add up to wasted time that could be more profitably spent, to say nothing of actually detracting from your natural beauty.

*e. The Wife's Parents:* By including this thought in our lesson we do not for one moment suggest that the young woman love her parents less than she formerly did. In the Bible we learn that we are to honor our parents and be concerned about their welfare as long as they live. And that means even after we leave their home to establish our own. But the kind of association with them to which I am referring in this study is that association that keeps you at your parents' home, or they at yours, for hours each day. The major attachment should be to your husband. Above all, if you and your husband should have a slight difference of opinion, don't take it to anyone. More especially don't take it "home to mother," for sympathy and understanding. I was fortunate in having a mother who was much wiser than I. Early in my marriage I made the mistake of taking a personal problem to her, a difference of opinion between my husband and me. Much to my surprise she sided with him. I never found out how she *really* felt. It was the last time I made that mistake. And, just in passing, I should like to mention that I am of the firm conviction that any christian, relying on God and his word, can settle any problem that might come up, whether it be with husband, children, stranger, regardless of the problem, if she will but go to the word of God for her answer. If God has not covered every phase of our lives it would mean he had given us an inadequate guide, and I do not for one moment think that is so. Surely it must be a lack of faith, ignorance of the word, or a sign of weakness on the part of any child of God when he thinks that someone who knows nothing about God's word, nor cares, can give us a better answer to our problems than God has already done in his word. Learn to work out your own answers, you and your husband together, by prayer and a thorough study of what

God has revealed to us.

*f. Money and Success:* Earning the money and gaining the success in life that goes with leadership is the realm that belongs to the husband. The young wife will not be overly concerned about it. You should be interested in his problems, sympathetic toward his failures, and full of praise for his achievements. But your main concern is not in the realm of finance nor achievement. Be willing to conform to his planning for the best way in which he may achieve this success. The planning should be his.

*g. Careers, Talents, Activities:* Should a woman have a career? If she has inborn talents such as the ability to paint, play an instrument, and do any kind of art work, should she pursue those fields? Should activities outside the home, such as worthy causes, club meetings, societies, P.T.A. meetings, art classes of any kind, be hers to enjoy? Yes, yes, yes to all three. In another section of this same lesson we will discuss in more detail just when, and under what circumstances these activities could be right. Suffice it to say under this particular heading that a wife should enter into no amount of activities that would detract from the primary purpose she has in making and maintaining a good home life. Our study in this particular lesson is to set forth as a *bad* example the wife who is so engrossed in outside activities (not particularly necessary) that she is never at home, never has time for the husband, never has time to cook good meals nor take proper care of her children. This is exceeding the proper allotment of time that should be spent on outside activities.

### Are You To Be Number One With Your Husband?

Yes, you should rate first with your husband *if* we are talking about his reason for working, for achieving, for living. But because of the nature of this his work, his duty to provide, his interest and responsibility for his job will demand more of his thinking, his waking hours than the actual time he may have to devote to you. In his over-all planning for his family his greatest concern should be for the family. But in accomplishing this aim he cannot always make the family first, time-wise, or even in his thoughts. Good wives will not begrudge him this interest in his work. They will realize that

36

when they take second place in his time allotment, the wives lose nothing. Let me emphasize the fact that this is especially so in some lines of work. A doctor, for instance, will be called upon at the most unscheduled moments of the day or night. To a dedicated doctor an anniversary or a birthday celebration means absolutely nothing in comparison. The Hippocratic oath that he has taken when entering into the medical profession demands of him first allegiance to his patients' needs. The same is true, and even more important, in the life of a preacher of the gospel. The primary work of an evangelist is the preaching of the gospel and the salvation of the souls of men. Nothing can approach the seriousness of this charge. Paul tells Timothy, a young preacher, "Preach the word: be urgent in season, out of season . . ." (2 Timothy 4:2). That simply means when it is convenient and when it is not. So many times my husband has gone at the wee hours of the morning, or the late hours of the night, to comfort and console a loved one when death or serious illness had come to the family. Requests from any for his time must have priority. To my knowledge I cannot recall that in the years he has preached he has ever turned down a single invitation to come teach, with one exception for illness. This includes both congregations and individuals. On many of these occasions, something else had been planned, but the plans had to be changed. Surely every dedicated preacher will have this same attitude. The wife of a preacher must understand this. If she does not there is bound to be trouble in the offing.

The same attitude toward priorities must be held by dedicated elders in the church, or any other such important work. As far as the work of good elders is concerned I guess only their wives can fully realize the amount of hours consumed by them as they strive to carry out their responsibilities for their flock. This is as it should be and every right-thinking wife should be prepared for this eventuality in her life. No greater or more sobering work can be found than the responsibility of elders. Every wife should be happy to have a part like this in the molding of the lives of both her husband and herself into the promise of a work in the church.

## His Natural Role As Guide

The guide for the family is a God-given role, given to the man. He is adequately equipped for this position. Men are born leaders. To wives God said, "Wives, be in subjection unto your own husbands, as unto the Lord. For the husband is the head of the wife, as Christ also is the head of the church, being himself the saviour of the body. But as the church is subject to Christ, so let the wives also be to their husbands in everything" (Ephesians 5:22-24).

The first commandment God gave to woman after her fall was ". . . thy desire shall be to thy husband and he shall rule over thee" (Genesis 3:16). Paul said, "Let the wife see that she fear her husband" (Ephesians 5:33). Again Paul said, "Wives, be in subjection to your husbands, *as is fitting in the Lord*" (Colossians 3:18). Peter said the same thing, "In like manner, ye wives, be in subjection to your own husbands" (1 Peter 3:1)

Women are the weaker vessels. Why should I make a claim like this? Because Peter said, "Ye husbands, in like manner, dwell with your wives according to knowledge, giving honor (idiom: support) unto the woman, *as unto the weaker vessel,* as being joint-heirs of the grace of life; to the end that your prayers be not hindered" (1 Peter 3:7).

In what respect are women the weaker vessels? Is it physically? Perhaps in the general sense of "strength" men have more brute strength than do women, though this is not true in every case. Yet insurance companies know that women will outlive men. In your daily work around the home, tending babies, cooking, washing, ironing, I know that a woman's endurance is amazing. It would be difficult for a man to surpass a woman in this realm. So in the physical realm a woman is not weaker.

What about her mentality? Is she weaker mentally? Ask any school teacher. The girls make as good grades as do the boys, are equally as bright and alert. They perhaps apply themselves better than do boys. A little girl said to a little boy: "Did you know that girls are smarter than boys?" "No, I didn't know that!" "You see!" she came back. All joking aside I am sure you would agree that the mentality of girls and boys, women and men, is equal.

Are women weaker spiritually? Look up and down any church pew. Women outnumber men. They have just as great a sense of spirituality as any man. They love the Lord just as much. So the realm of spirituality is not the greater weakness.

Then in what respect are women the weaker vessels? I would say it is in the realm of emotionalism. Women are not as stable as men; they tend to vacillate. They cannot make up their minds by themselves. They are much more easily persuaded than men.

Think about how women could be swayed through emotionalism if she were given positions of leadership in the church or nation. If an eloquent speaker should stand before a group of men and women and make an impassioned plea for a poor family in dire need, it would be the women who were touched rather than the men. He paints a picture of sick children with no food, no clothing, insufficient bedding, and a sick husband unable to work. He then asks that a contribution be taken for them. Granting that the women had in their possession a like amount of money and were answerable to no one but themselves for it, from whom do you think the greatest contribution would come? I think from the women. Men tend to sit in judgment, being more critical and skeptical than women. They would ask themselves questions like, "How did the family get in this shape? Do they have any close relatives who should be helping them?" Women give before they rationalize. Suppose situations like this came before the church (as indeed they do) and women were acting as elders. Think how they could be touched into helping in situations where perhaps they should not.

This is a good spot to discuss some of the unbalanced ideas of the women's liberation movement abroad in our country today. Women who do not know that God said He knows our frame and knows what is best for us, who do not know and perhaps do not care about the role in which God has placed women are making statements contrary to God's arrangement. They want equal rights for women. Equal in what respect? If a woman does the same job a man does, she should be paid the same salary. Any right-thinking person acknowledges this. Our law is already in force on this point. But women want more than that. They want positions men now occupy whether they are qualified or not. They want to look like a man, act like a man, do everything a man does. That is against nature. I believe God knows what is best for us and I believe that God knows our nature better than we know our own. Based on this belief, I am willing to state that women are letting themselves in for untold difficulties, The wheel of nature is being sadly unbalanced. If we would be willing to follow God's plan we (women) will benefit, men will benefit, children will benefit, and our nation will benefit. All mankind is thus made happier and better.

Think for a moment about how rewarding a woman's work is in the home, particularly in the raising of sons to positions of leadership in the world. Think what a great privilege is yours to be able to raise sons to be preachers or elders in the Lord's church. Next to that in importance would be to raise sons who would rise to powerful positions as great statesmen in our country. How we need them!

I heard a great old preacher tell a moving story once about holding a meeting in a little rural community. He was very disappointed in the results of that meeting. When asked about responses he replied, "One little girl, a teen-ager, was the only person who obeyed the gospel." Years later, after that little girl had grown to womanhood, she married, converted her husband, and from that union were born sons and daughters, all members of the church. Some became elders, some preachers, and wives of preachers and elders. What a far-reaching influence upon the lives of people was the response to the gospel of that one young lady. If we as women are successful in raising our children to have respect and love for the church so that they desire to be leaders in it, we have fulfilled the greatest role available to women. I personally think Paul's teaching is in keeping with the above statement when he said, "Let a woman learn in quietness with all subjection. But I permit not a woman to teach, nor to have dominion over a man, but to be in quietness. For Adam was first formed, then Eve: and Adam was not beguiled, but the woman being beguiled hath fallen into transgression: but she

40

shall be saved through her childbearing, if they continue in faith and love and sanctification with sobriety" (1 Timothy 2:11-15). In other words, if the woman fulfills her God-given role as the home-maker, teacher and guide of her children she will have done her duty toward God, will have raised herself from that state into which she had fallen through her sin, and will thus be saved eternally. She also will have given to the world Godly men and women.

## Why Man Should Be The Leader

As man performs his functions as a leader, he would like to think he does so with greater skill than a woman can attain. He does not desire to be in competition to her. He does not strive to excel her in domestic duties, or as a mother, or in any of the feminine roles. So why are women so persistent in trying to excel him in any of the masculine roles? He has duties as a leader to determine the policies, the rules and the laws for his family to follow. Contrary to some of the modern philosophies abroad in our land today the family is not a democracy where everybody votes and where the child's vote counts for as much as the parents'. Just as the church is not a democracy and we do not make the laws that govern the church, just that surely Paul said, "For the husband is the head of the wife, *as Christ also is the head of the church.*" This surely states emphatically that just as the church has a head, a ruler, so also the family. In some churches not governed by what Paul said open business meetings are held. Women, children and men who are not chosen leaders are invited to attend. Their voice in matters relating to the business of the church is heard on an equal with the voice of the elders. Nothing but chaos can come of such an arrangement as this. The same is true of the family. Children do not have the judgment to make the right decisions. Though a wise father will consider suggestions from any member of the family, it does not necessarily mean that he will adopt that suggestion. Wise elders will accept suggestions from any member of the church and will seriously consider it. Perhaps they will adopt the suggestion; perhaps not. In either case, wise fathers and elders give serious consideration to such suggestions, and if found worthy will generously give credit to the one making the suggestion. But the actual decision-making must be his, and our place is to acknowledge this fact, accept his decisions with grace.

Successful businesses are run on this same principle. They use suggestions from all employees, and even have suggestion boxes. If a suggestion is accepted, praise and honor goes to the one making the suggestion. This does not mean that this employee is running the business, and is on a par with the president or manager. Even though the suggestion is accepted, the decision to do so rests with the top man.

Women make a mistake in trying to take over the role of leader in the home. She might try to "rule the roost." Some ludicrous attempts at humor have been tried in order to explain a woman's "ruling the roost." They say, "Oh, yes, he is the head, but I am the neck, and the neck turns the head." That may be funny, but it should not be true of you.

Another mistake is in the field of advising. You should not have the attitude that you know more about it than he, and that if he does not take your advice he is in big trouble. Can you accept defeat when your advice is not accepted?

If trying to give advice does not work, some women will try all manner of schemes to pressure the man into doing what she wants done. They threaten, they insist, they nag, they cry, they throw a temper tantrum, they accuse their husbands of not loving them, and they withhold affection as a means of punishment.

Finally, if all these fail, they just outright disobey. They did not get their way, and they are determined to do so at any expense. So they go ahead and do what they wanted to do in the first place. This is in direct violation of God's law. God said for the wife to be in subjection. We no more have the right to disobey this law of God than we do any other law. Think about it when you are so tempted.

## Questions On
## LESSON NO. 4

### Man As The Leader

1. Name two qualities which were studied in this lesson that men desire to possess?

2. What should be your attitude if he should meet with a set-back?

3. Why does he need to be number one?

4. What are some of the mistakes wives make in denying him position number one?

5. Give your evaluation of the allotment of your time between your husband and your children.

6. How can you spend too much time taking care of the home?

7. How can you reach a happy medium on time spent on personal appearance?

8. To what extent are your parents entitled to your time and attention?

9. Should a wife be concerned about money and success?

10. Should a woman's time be devoted to establishing her career? What about her natural talents, and outside activities?

11. Name a realm in which the husband should be head man. Quote scriptures.

12. Should a man make his wife the foremost interest time-wise?

13. In what respect do you think woman is the weaker vessel? Discuss the various fields.

14. How does women's lib destroy the balance of nature in the realm of husband-wife relationship?

15. Is the home a democracy, where everybody votes? Name something else that is not a democracy. Why does this make common sense?

16. Give some ways in which women try to take over the reins as leader.

# "To Love Their Husbands"

### Problems To Be Dealt With

Since we have learned that man's role is that of leader, there may be circumstances and situations that will present some real, not imaginary problems for you. These will have to be worked out. For instance:

1. You may be married to a man who is really wicked. He has no interest in things spiritual. He will not listen, will be inclined not to be influenced by what you say or do. I am hoping that all girls not yet married will be very sure that the man she plans to marry is not of that character. But how does one know beforehand? It is very difficult to know a man thoroughly in a short period of time. Some people are perceptive enough to see some clues that will point in certain directions. One of the best ways to avoid this bad situation is to become acquainted with him before marriage. By "acquainted" we do not mean a mere "how-do-you-do?" acquaintance. We mean become familiar with his moods. Watch out for unguarded moments when you may catch him off-guard in his language, his actions, his plans for your future life together. Watch him around children, around old people. How does he react to ticklish situations? You have heard good advice from your elders to the effect that when a boy is courting a girl he is on his best behaviour. Do not assume that in a short courtship he will reveal every facet of his

personality. This is one of the best arguments for a long courtship. Be with him long enough to find out if there *is* another side and thus prevent a lifetime of unhappiness.

In case you do not discover bad qualities before marriage, but do find out after marriage, what can a christian young woman do about it? If at all possible, live with him. If he will allow you to keep your commitments to God, to worship, to attend classes, to have the fellowship of other christians, then I suppose you would be obligated to make the best of a bad situation.

2. There could be another situation in marriage that is as bad as the one portrayed above. A man could be a good provider, attentive to you, and good to the children when things were going good, but when in certain moods could be cruel and vicious. Wife-beating is a prevalent crime in the United States, much more prevalent than statistics show because many wives will not report such beatings. They do not because they are ashamed or afraid of later reprisals. Sometimes the wife-beater is apprehended but cannot be brought to trial because the wife refuses to press charges against him. In such situations as this one, first be very sure you are not just imagining his cruelty. Some wives think if their husbands draw the pursestrings a little tighter this constitutes cruelty. It may be they need drawing tighter. Again some wives can nag, cut a man down with snide remarks and mentally torture a man into some extreme actions like suddenly striking out at her. If he had not been pressured he would not have considered doing such a thing; it was a momentary reaction. Be sure that any physical abuse is not your fault. But if you are being a proper wife and he still shows tendencies of abuse for no reason, you are not required to submit to this abuse. Deal with it, or leave him.

3. Is he a poor manager? This situation can likely be an imaginary one. Wives sometimes have the tendency to think husbands cannot handle situations as well as they themselves can. Wives think the husbands will make mistakes. Well they almost certainly will! Who doesn't? Wives make mistakes, too, in judgment and in actual performance, but we learn from our mistakes. We would not like it if our husbands decided we

were not competent to cook a meal, do the shopping, or perform other duties of a wife simply because we made a mistake. There have been instances in our knowledge when the man so decided and took over these duties himself. The wife was no longer "queen of her home" but a mere slave. Just as he was out of line so would you be if you assumed the role of the husband for fear he would make a mistake. He will, but he can overcome and will thus become the wiser and stronger for it. Step out of this role, if you have assumed it, and don't make the mistake of thinking only you can handle decisions.

4. Strangely, husbands are like people! They do not always have successes. Failures will come to them as well as to you. At those times he will have a tendency to become down-hearted and blue. He will consider doing other things, getting into another line of work. These are the times when the wife, if she is wise, will lend encouragement rather than discouragement. Do everything you can to aid him, not further tear him down.

There will be times like this when it would be very easy for you to step in and assume the role of the leader. Some men by nature are better equipped to lead than others, and if you should be married to one who does not lead naturally you would be further tempted to assume the role. Probably in your observations of other marriages you have witnessed just such marriages. The domineering wife who leads her husband about by the nose; a milk-toast kind of man who comes and goes at her beck and call. It presents a disgusting picture to the world and certainly does not conform to any kind of union God has designed for his children.

My husband has a particular aversion to the television shows that portray the husband and father as some kind of nincompoop. He provides the necessities but that is as far as his role goes. Every decision is made by either the wife or the children. When any comedy situation comes up it is always the father who is the fall guy, the brunt of every joke. Watching these kinds of portrayals of family life makes a deep impression on the youngsters, an impression of the father taking the back seat in home management and planning. No wonder the world has accepted a reverse role. Women today should be the first to encourage him to take the lead, rather than trying to take over that role for themselves.

But just suppose he refuses to assume his role, especially after he has failed at whatever he is doing? What can you do to keep out of that role? Well, you will have a job on your hands, but it can be done. You can show him by your actions that you have confidence in him. You can let go the reins and let him know that you expect him to lead. You can sit down with him and read the passages of scriptures that teach him to assume the role of leadership. Little by little you can again build up his confidence in himself.

Together you can pray fervently for wisdom to adjust to situations. Just suppose that he wants to do one thing but you have your mind set on doing another. What do you do in that circumstance? First, I would suggest that you develop the proper attitude toward adaptability, toward not getting your way. There is nothing wrong in expressing your ideas for his consideration; in fact, I think it is wise. But when you do you should also convince him that you are willing for him to make the final decision. When he sees that your attitude is right, that you are willing to go along with his decisions, this will do much to help him in building up his confidence in himself.

One thing I would stress: whatever disagreements you may have, thrash them out between the two of you, come to a decision, and present a united front to the children. Children are intelligent; they catch on fast. It doesn't take them long to learn to play one parent against the other if they are divided. They will go to the one who says yes to them. Even if you disagree about a decision the other has made, do not let the children see this.

## II. PROTECTING

Protection! Does a woman really need protection in our modern society? When "knighthood was in flower" the role of protector was most graphically portrayed. Men fought duels for the young ladies and protected their honor with their lives. But even now the role of protector flourishes in our own society. Men are especially adapted to fulfill this role. Men enjoy the role of the protector. It awakens chivalry in

48

them. We dream about our men being chivalrous but we seldom give them the opportunity, because we are so set on being independent. Women need protection today from many things. There are dangers lurking all about us: sexual assault and threat to life; strenuous work, too hard for the woman; difficulties that men can overcome but that women do not know how to handle.

This is another area in which women's liberation movement becomes a farce. Women are *not* equipped to protect themselves from many situations. Fanciful thinking that she can does not make it so. But if women's lib has its way, the beautiful chivalrous attitude men display toward women will become a thing of the past. How sad that day! How women will desire to have it back! It can become lost to them forever unless they awaken to what they are wreaking.

It has always been true in every age that men enjoy protecting girls and women. When boys are small they scare little girls by threatening them with snakes, frogs, worms and spiders. Girls shriek and run, and boys chase. Nobody has told them this is the "proper" order of things. It is a very natural tendency. As boys and girls grow into adulthood the boy wants to protect his girl from just those very things with which he once tried to frighten her. It gives him great satisfaction to comfort and soothe her when she has been frightened by any situation. This again is a natural reaction, and one that needs to be cultivated rather than stifled. In marriage this same quality of protective care is seen in how husbands wish to shelter their wives from disagreeable duties and responsibilities. What a wonderful life for a wife to have this protection! It should serve as a source of great enjoyment to her rather than something she would want to squelch in him. Watch as the protective husband opens the car door for his beloved mate, how he carries in the heavy sacks of groceries, changes the flat tire, takes care of heavy tasks around the house. Can any right-thinking woman wish to have it any other way? Would you feel good about doing those difficult tasks while the husband stood by and watched you perform? Frankly, I would hate for our roles to change so drastically.

## III. PROVIDING

Going along with guiding the household and protecting is the role of providing. To Adam God gave the charge, "Cursed is the ground for thy sake; in toil shalt thou eat of it all the days of thy life; thorns also and thistles shall it bring forth to thee; in the sweat of thy face shalt thou eat bread, till thou return unto the ground . . ." (Genesis 3:17-19). Man innately wants to feel needed in this role. He does not appreciate the wife who feels that she must help him provide for the family in order to give them something he cannot supply. It destroys his manly pride and makes him feel inadequate to the situation. Man needs to function in this role, to feel needed.

In the Bible the stress is always on *man*, not *woman*, as the breadwinner. The above verses in Genesis 3 clearly state this principle. In the New Testament, Paul teaches the same thing, when he admonished, "But if any *provideth not for his own*, and especially *his own household*, he hath denied the faith, and is worse than an unbeliever" (1 Timothy 5:8). Again, Paul said, "For even when we were with you, this we commanded you, If any will not work, neither let him eat" (2 Thessalonians 3:10).

What, then, should a man provide? He is under obligation to provide the *necessities of life*. What does this include? It includes food, shelter, and clothing. Man is under no obligation to provide luxuries, but may, if circumstances give him that opportunity, and he so desires. There may be economies under which people are required to live that prevents a man from providing anything but necessities. Women sometimes forget this, if they ever knew it. Their minds become so cluttered with the "things" of this life until they actually feel "put upon" if the husband does not lavish the luxuries upon them, providing them with every new invention on the market. Try to remember under trying circumstances that he loves you and would like to be able to give you every luxury you want, but probably is not financially able to do so. If you keep in mind that the luxuries are not the necessary things, and that when they come, if ever they do, it is out of the goodness of his heart that he gives them, you will face realities with the proper frame of mind.

## Should Women Work?

In our modern society this topic will demand some soul-searching, much honesty in your own heart, and a thorough study of God's word on this important subject. I am sure that each one of you, reading this, will say within your mind, "I know a woman in the church who works, and if she can, why cannot I?" Let us resolve now to forever quell the disposition of mind that rationalizes any situation. Just suppose that the teacher of your Bible class works? that three of the elders' wives work? that the preacher's wife works? Just suppose that your own mother works? Is that the basis upon which this question or any other Bible subject should be settled? Then what is the source of authority? God's word! This is the basis for *all* the answers to *all* our questions.

With this foundation in mind, we would like to present some instances in the word of God where women worked, and see if we can draw a proper conclusion from what God has to say about it:

There was a woman named Deborah. She was a prophetess of God, dwelt under a palm tree and judged the children of Israel who came to her. This she did with the approval and sanction of God (Judges 4:1-9).

Again in the Old Testament we read of another prophetess, Huldah. She dwelt in Jerusalem, in the temple grounds. Priests and elders of the Israelites came to her for counsel of God, and she gave it (2 Kings 22:14-20).

Going to the New Testament, we learn about Aquila and his wife Priscilla, Jews from Rome who were dwelling in Corinth. They were tentmakers by trade, and Priscilla worked alongside her husband in this business. She was approved of God (Acts 18:1-3).

Another woman who evidently had a lucrative business was Lydia, a seller of purple. Paul found her in Philippi, taught her, and she obeyed the gospel. Nothing was said about discontinuing her work in the business world (Acts 16:14).

Paul said about a good woman, "I commend unto you Phoebe, our sister, who is a servant of the church that is at

51

Cenchreae, that ye receive her in the Lord, worthily of the saints, and that ye assist her in whatsoever matter she may have need of you: for she herself hath also been a helper of many, and of mine own self" (Romans 16:1).

Later on in this same chapter Paul mentions Priscilla again as being one who laid down her life for Paul's sake; and of Mary, who bestowed much labor on them.

From these instances in the word of God of working women, we can see that working, in and of itself, is not wrong. Then is there anything about it that would condemn it? Yes, there could be, if the motive for working was wrong. We will discuss these motives later, but first, let us examine some of the *good* reasons women should be able to give for working outside the home.

That woman is an intelligent being no sane person could deny. Many times her education and training would enable her to hold down a good job. But when she marries she changes the course of her life. She has now assumed the responsibility of a husband, a home, and in most cases of children. An intelligent woman will apply herself to this new life as diligently as she would to a position outside her home. It is a full-time job, and requires the best we have in order to perform acceptably. But circumstances sometimes alter our plans, and we have to do the best we can under adverse circumstances. Some of these circumstances might be:

• Your husband's illness over a long period of time. He may have suffered a stroke, may have had a severe heart attack, or a lingering illness such as cancer or any other crippling disease that would render him incapable of working. It is imperative, and hopefully possible, that the wife find a job to sustain the family.

• Another reason might be a business set-back, in which case the wife could work temporarily until the business could be set on its feet again.

• Imagine a situation where your husband becomes aware that his education is not sufficient to further him in his chosen field. Or perhaps he wants to go into another line of work but lacks the necessary education to do so. Both he and you agree that it would be good if you worked, tempor-

52

arily, to enable him to get the education he needs. Your working would certainly be justified for this reason.

• Then there are those rare instances where the older woman finds her pressing household duties lessened. The children are grown and married, the husband is still active and busy in his work, and you suddenly find yourself with time on your hands. Along comes a good offer, either for part-time or full-time work. I see nothing wrong with this arrangement if you will allow me these qualifying statements:

It is hard for me to imagine a woman with "time on her hands." It may be that my life is vastly different from the majority, in that I am the wife of a preacher. My husband, even in retirement from local work, is still actively engaged in working with people and in preaching the gospel. I find it most difficult to have "time on my hands." Even if you do not have the same demands on your time, think what a blessing you could be to the church if you wisely used time you never had before. Many times in your busy years you made the statement, "If I had the time, I would make a thorough study of the history of the Old Testament. If I had the time, I would attend every Bible class I could. If I had the time, I would sew, knit, crochet or cook for someone who really needs it." Well, now you have the time. Did you really mean it when you said it, or was that just idle talk? Make a place in your schedule for time to visit the sick and infirm; to attend all the classes possible; to take food to sorrowing families. You will find your life richly rewarded. You will become a better person, a better student, a happy individual thinking of doing for others rather than becoming old, senile and bitter.

We said before that the motive behind a woman's working outside the home would determine whether or not it was justified. This is an area in which you must be very honest with yourself. Search your own heart. Hopefully you will come up with the right answer.

Some wrong motives for working might be:

▪ To supply the luxuries your husband has not been able to provide for you. This is a terrific blow to a man's pride. He knows that you are saying to him, "You are not capable of giving me what I want."

■ You are bored with life, and you seek fulfillment. This excuse is no reason at all, and can be overcome. There are many ways of relieving boredom. Some were suggested before, but let's look at a few of the ways in which boredom can be relieved:

— Learning is a thrilling experience. The more one learns the more one wants to learn. Get interested in an in-depth study of the Bible. Most people are content with a smattering of knowledge of God's word. In the sermon on the mount Jesus said the people would be happy (blessed) who *hungered* and *thirsted* after righteousness, or in other words, after a knowledge of God's word. What an expressive way to state the idea that a study of God's word should be diligently pursued, and thus enjoyed. If you were on a desert, lost, stranded, the hot sun beating down upon you, what would be your greatest desire in this world? Water, of course. You can even imagine that you see it when you begin to hallucinate. A craving thirst comes over you, driving you almost mad. You would do anything to get that drink of water. That is the same thirst a child of God should have for the word of God. It is a rare thing to see a person who really applies herself to a thorough and systematic study of the Bible. You would be richly rewarded if you did.

— Another way to avoid boredom is to interest yourself in teaching others. Learn something to teach, first of all, and then apply yourself to teaching your neighbors. There are many young women I know who have set up classes with their friends. This is good, and this activity will give you a wholesome outlook on life, alleviate your boredom, and at the same time be a blessing to you and them.

— In the realm of the mundane, you could pursue classes in decorating, gardening, or other worthwhile projects to make your home life more interesting and profitable.

— What about getting interested in helping old people? There are many old people in nursing homes who would love to have you visit them. They need not be of your acquaintance. Some people have nobody to visit them at all. We have gone to homes to visit people we know, and have found many perfect strangers who speak to us, and want you to speak to them. Make these people part of your visits, learn their names, find out something about their lives, and give them something to which they can look forward every so often, your visit.

— There are things about your husband's business that might prove interesting to you if you would take the interest and time to learn it. It would give you an insight into his life that you might never had had before. You and he could more intelligently talk over his problems.

— Politics is not a dirty word. A great many of our politicians have made it so, and there are very few statesmen anymore. But still there are some areas in which you could serve your country well if you would be interested in getting involved in some phases of politics. In this realm I would advise limited participation, to say the least.

■ Another very poor excuse for working outside the home is "to ease the load for the man." First of all, does it need easing? Is there some good reason that he needs your financial help, such as the ones we discussed earlier? Honestly now, is it just to "ease the load for yourself?"

The *HARM* that could derive from your working could offset all the good it might accomplish. If there are children at home, they would be left without your oversight. Oh yes, you have provided a baby sitter. Perhaps you are fortunate enough to have found an excellent one. But do you think that baby-sitter can give them what you can give them? Think of the many times that a child comes home from school and calls for you. He wants to know you are there. Right at that instant he might have a question that is important to him. He wants to ask *you.* But you are not there, you are working. That moment forever slips away and the opportunity you might have had to put something worthwhile into that child's mind is gone forever.

Another harm that I definitely see in working out is that it can develop within the woman a sense of independence that would be detrimental to the relationship ordained by God between husband and wife. The husband is in the role of leader and breadwinner, the wife in the role of homemaker. The working wife changes that relationship and becomes almost entirely independent of his role of provider. When she does this she then expects him to help her perform the duties which were previously hers alone. This can create all sorts of problems as to the proper distribution of the work load. Many marriages flounder just here at this point.

Within our society the world has come to see the result of women going into the job market in great numbers since World War II. The need for women workers during that time, with men in the service, has brought about a continuation of their desire to earn money and be independent. A revolution of the work load has occurred internationally. The social upheaval caused by so many jobs being filled by women, the threat to economic security, and the lack of jobs open to men as a result have brought about the development of most threatening economic problems, social upheaval, divorce, violence on the streets and on campuses, drug abuse, rebellion against social customs and moral standards. Though I do not make the claim that all problems in our society today can be attributed to the working women, I do avow that this enters into the picture as a looming threat, and needs correcting. I am sorry to say that I do not see in our society now a return to the kind of life we once knew. "Baby, you've come a long way" is now so true, unfortunately, and so disgusting, that I cannot foresee a change in the future. I would hope that in time the pendulum will swing, and that there will be an about-face.

### Man's Need For Fulfillment of Natural Appetites

The last point we will study under man's needs is one to which we should give grave and serious study.

Every appetite man has on this earth has a legitimate means by which it can be satisfied. Hunger, a natural appetite, can be satisfied legitimately by earning money to buy food. We do not, should not, steal to satisfy that urge illegitimately.

Man has another appetite, his need for sexual relationship with a woman. As we have discussed previously, this relationship cannot be satisfied legitimately outside the marriage relationship. But it is a beautiful thing if lawfully satisfied in this way God has legislated. The writer of Hebrews said, "Let marriage be had in honor among all, and let the bed be undefiled: for fornicators and adulterers God will

56

judge" (Hebrews 13:4). Women, do not make the mistake of withholding sex from your husband for the purpose of punishing him for some slight, whether imagined or real. Sex between husband and wife should not be so used. The main thing to be remembered is that you love each other, that you are a natural complement to each other's needs, and that you want this very intimate relationship to continue as long as desire continues. Do not misuse it, nor abuse it. This will cause both him and you untold years of happiness.

## Additional Thoughts

One other thing I would stress in a woman's relationship to her husband is this: In many instances a christian finds herself married to a man who is not a christian. First of all, before marriage I would stress that you find a man who *is* a member of the church. That in itself would eliminate many problems you would otherwise have to solve. But if you do find yourself with a mate who cares nothing for the word of God or its teaching, remember that your first allegiance is to God.

New Testament writers, guided by the inspiration of the Holy Spirit, have taught us to be in obedience to civil authority. But the implication is clear that we should obey God first. If civil authorities command us to do anything that conflicts with what God has commanded, then God comes first. Peter and John had been commanded by the authorities not to speak at all, nor to teach in the name of Jesus. Peter answered, "Whether it is right in the sight of God to hearken unto you *rather* than unto God, judge ye: for we cannot but speak the things which we saw and heard" (Acts 4:18-20).

So, if your husband should charge you to not attend services, to not attend classes, to not live a clean, moral life, but rather to go with him into the bars or on week-end trips where you could not worship, or to stay with him when Bible classes are being conducted, or in any way betray the charge given you by God when you obeyed the gospel, your first allegiance is to God.

Another interesting thing about doing what is right about this is the fact that when you do obey God rather than man, your husband will be more apt to see that there is really something to what you have espoused. Remember, God knows our frame, He knows the things that are good for us, and He has not asked us to do anything that is not good for us. If you continue to serve the Lord faithfully and quietly (read 1 Peter 3:2) this will do more to win your husband to Christ than anything you can do. But if you compromise with him and yield to his demands he will quickly see that the thing you have espoused is really not very important to you either, and would thus be discouraged in accepting it himself.

## Questions On
## LESSON NO. 5

**Some Real Problems You May Encounter**

1. Why should a young girl become thoroughly acquainted with a man before agreeing to marry him?

2. How are some of the ways a girl can detect that a man is not all he claims to be?

3. If, after marriage, you find you are married to a wicked person, what should be your responsibility?

4. In the event a husband turns out to be a wife-beater, what is the best way to handle this situation?

5. When he makes mistakes in judgment, or in actual performance, what should a wife do?

6. When he actually fails, what then?

7. If he will not lead, what can the wife do about following?

8. Name other ways you can go about encouraging him to accept his leadership role.

**Protector and Provider**

9. From what things does modern woman need protection?

10. How can we learn to accept his protection?

11. To whom did God give the role of "bread-winner?" Quote passage.

12. What things are men obligated to provide? What things are they not?

## The Working Wife

13. Name some of the women of the Bible who worked, and give quotations.

14. Under what circumstances would a woman be justified in holding down a full time job?

15. When is the working wife not justified?

16. Think of some of the ways in which harm could come by your working.

17. Discuss man's need for sexual fulfillment.

18. In being obedient to your husband, is someone higher than he? If so, who?

19. Under what circumstances would a wife be justified in not obeying her husband?

# "To Love Their Children"

The blessings of motherhood! "Lo, children are an heritage of the Lord: and the fruit of the womb is his (her) reward" (Psalms 127:3).

Though the blessings of motherhood are accompanied by great and grave responsibilities, the role of motherhood provides woman with the opportunity to fulfill her God-given role in life. It can be a great and rewarding work, and can bring to the nation men that are qualified to handle grave problems of national character. How the world needs men of character, those who are motivated by a real belief in the word of God, who will not lie, cheat, nor misrepresent. The founders of our great nation, though not many of them were christians, were motivated by a love for the word of God. Many of the precepts taught in the Bible became the foundation stones for the great documents, the Constitution and the Bill of Rights. Leaders often referred to the Bible when called upon to make speeches. Our civil law was based on precepts taught in the word of God. When nations, as well as individuals, forsake these precepts, that nation and that individual is on the downward road. His digression is sure and final.

"Righteousness exalteth a nation; but sin is a reproach to any people" (Proverbs 14:34).

"Blessed (happy) is the nation whose God is Jehovah . . ."

(Psalms 33:12).

And, finally, "The wicked shall be turned back unto Sheol, even all the nations that forget God" (Psalms 9:17). The United States is no exception to this rule. Consider the great world powers that existed in the past. The historian, Gibbon, gave as the reasons for the fall of Rome:

• The rapid increase of divorce, with the undermining of the home, which is the basis of society.

• Higher and higher taxes; the spending of public money for bread and celebrations.

• The mad craze for pleasure; sports becoming every year more exciting and more brutal.

• The building of gigantic armaments, when the real enemy was within; the decadence of the people.

• The decay of religion; faith fading into mere form, losing touch with life, and becoming impotent to guide it.

*[Decline and Fall of the Roman Empire]*

Professor Alexander Tyler, over 200 years ago, while our thirteen original colonies still belonged to Great Britain, wrote of the Fall of the Athenian republic of over 2000 years before:

"A democracy cannot exist as a permanent form of government. It can only exist until the voters discover that they can vote themselves largesse from the public treasury. From that moment on, the majority always votes for the candidates promising them the most benefits . . .

"The average age of the world's greatest civilizations has been 200 years. These nations have progressed through this sequence:

1. From bondage to spiritual faith.
2. From spiritual faith to great courage.
3. From courage to liberty.
4. From liberty to abundance.
5. From abundance to selfishness.
6. From selfishness to complacency.
7. From complacency to apathy.
8. From apathy to dependency.
9. From dependency back again into bondage."

We have elected officials who will give us the handout today. We sadly need leaders who understand that God said,

"If a man will not work, neither let him eat" (2 Thessalonians 3:10).

Not only our nation but the church can be benefited by godly men, trained in the home by godly parents, and of course this is much more important. The church as given us by our Lord is perfect in its concept and design. Christ wants his bride, the church, to be spotless and without blemish. One of the ways He has devised for seeing that the church remains pure is by the selection of wise and godly men to act as overseers of His people. Elders, deacons, teachers and preachers all have their place in this plan of keeping the church pure. The greatest work parents can do is to raise children to be workers in the church of the Lord.

The role of motherhood can bring to the church men that are qualified to be elders and deacons of this great institution, the church. It can bring to the ministry preachers that are dedicated, instructed in God's word, and willing and able to make the necessary sacrifices to such a work.

When we think of some of the women of the Bible we immediately are made aware of the fact that throughout the history of mankind we have good and bad examples. We can profit from both. Of the good examples, the first one we would think of is that of Mary, the mother of Jesus. What an announcement was made to Mary, that she would be the mother of Jesus Christ, without human conception! She had the fortitude to accept it and saw Jesus born, saw him grow to manhood, and followed him about in his personal ministry! Here was a privilege that has been the greatest a woman will ever know: to realize that she brought into the world the Son of God, and that by this birth, death and resurrection all mankind could be saved.

But other worthy examples come to our minds also: We think of Hannah, who was childless, whose story is told in 1 Samuel 1. She prayed constantly to God that she might have a child. She wanted him so much that she made a vow to God, saying, "O Jehovah of hosts, if thou wilt indeed look on the affliction of thy handmaid, and remember me, and not forget thy handmaid, but wilt give unto thy handmaid a man-child, then I will give him unto Jehovah all the days of his life, and there shall no razor come upon his head" (vs. 11). God granted Hannah her desire and Hannah bore a son named Samuel, who became the high priest of the Israelites, one of the greatest leaders Israel ever knew.

Sarah, who also was childless and barren, greatly desired a child. God granted this woman her wish and Isaac was born to Abraham and Sarah in their old age. It was through Isaac, the child of promise, that the Israelite nation came into being, and through whom Jesus Christ was born into the world.

In the New Testament, one of the finest examples of dedication is that of Eunice and Lois, the mother and grandmother of Timothy. Paul writes to the young preacher, Timothy, "Having been reminded of the unfeigned faith that is in thee; which dwelt first in thy grandmother Lois, and thy mother Eunice; and, I am persuaded, in thee also" (2 Timothy 1:5). What a joy it must have been for this godly mother to know that she had been instrumental in bringing Timothy to this point in his life, that he should receive such a commendation from the great apostle Paul.

Bad examples can be lessons for us, too: Examples such as the wicked queen over Israel, Jezebel. So wicked was she that her very name has come down to us as a byword to denote all that is evil, traitorous, designing and mean. She influenced her husband, Ahab, to be even more wicked than he was. She died a horrible death, as was prophesied by God. No one mourned her passing. We shy away from such examples as this and try to build our lives on the worthy examples of the Bible.

Before her children are born a woman should qualify herself to be the kind of mother God would have her to be. Some of the things we will mention will be of great help to young women. Reflect on the following ways in which you can prepare yourself for motherhood:

*1. Be prepared to give your time.* Time! that great instrument of good or of evil. There is just so much time in a twenty-four hour period, and every one of us has the same amount. How we divide our time, how much we apportion to various duties, is the great problem facing all of us. There are so many pressing duties, and each of us has her own. They may vary, but they are there.

Your husband needs a part of your time; the home requires a certain amount of your time; children demand their share of your time, and *you* need some time for yourself. How shall one separate the important things from the nonessential or trivial? Which comes first? How do we know what is best? Well, we don't always know. There is an old adage that says, "A stitch in time saves nine." But if you have just picked up a garment with needle and thread to take that one stitch, and suddenly realize your house is on fire, that definitely is not the time for that one stitch. I like the one in Ecclesiastes that says, "For everything there is a season, and a time for every purpose under heaven . . ." (Ecclesiastes 3:1).

A proper division of time is essential. But before marriage and before children come, learn this well: *you must be prepared to give of your time and self.* If you think getting married and having children is the way to get out of working and away from responsibilities, *think again!* They have just begun. From this moment on you will be responsible for things your parents took care of before. How well I recall the first time it dawned upon me that if it rained at night *I* was responsible for seeing that the windows were closed! Now that's a very trivial thing, but do you know that I did not have that responsibility before I married? And even greater surprises awaited me, I can assure you!

*2. Have a proper evaluation of what is important.* Put first things first. Try to strike a good balance in life. Your relationships are all important. We cannot stress too much the importance of keeping the relationship between you and your husband close and sweet. In this study today, however, and for a few lessons following, we will be stressing the training of your children. Any stress we place on any phase of these lessons does not exclude the other areas of responsibility. Make a time and a place for all of them, and in proper order. You may think this is an impossible task, and I am sure that at times it will seem so. But believe me, it has worked out successfully for many happy wives and mothers. And if they can do it, you can too.

*Among* the most important part of these responsibilities is the training of your children in the following areas: Spiritually, mentally, morally, and physically.

Part of the child's training, and a very early part, comes from your example as he watches you performing your duties relating to your home and husband. It teaches him by example that you have other interests. It teaches him that the home is important, and that being industriously occupied in your duties is a necessary part of your work. He learns and develops character from this example of industry. He learns that he is not the only pebble on the beach, and that mother must of necessity have other interests. From this he learns to share, to be unselfish, and that sometimes others come first. Character-building is not something that we learn from a set of rules, which a child learns to recite by memory. Rather, character-building is slowly etched on the child's mind by your example, your teaching, your everyday life until it becomes a part of him. His character slowly but surely is being formed over the impressionable years.

In striving to put first things first, remember that your own spiritual life is equally important, and that this must not be neglected to your own hurt. Remember the story of Mary and Martha? Remember that when Jesus came to their home, Martha went about getting things in readiness for the meal, while Mary sat at Jesus' feet to hear words of wisdom from his lips? This irked Martha, so she asked the Lord to bid Mary to help her. Jesus, with considerable kindness, said, "Martha, Martha, thou art anxious and troubled about many things: but one thing is needful: for Mary hath chosen the good part, which shall not be taken away from her" (Luke 10: 41,42). I remember an illustration given by brother Yater Tant in a sermon, in which he pointed out that many women try to do so much on Sunday morning that they rush into services, perhaps late, fall into a pew exhausted and have no strength with which to worship and praise God. What could they give in the way of service? That is not putting first things first. Arrange your time so that you can get things done ahead of time and have time left over for study, worship, spiritual growth and service to our Creator.

*3. The Child's Spiritual Training.* "Train up a child in the way he should go, and when he is old he will not depart from it" (Proverbs 22:6). The Proverbs is a book of wise sayings. A proverb is an adage, not a hard-and-fast-rule. I sometimes hear people say, "I knew a boy that was raised in a good home and he went bad; therefore that proverb is not true." No, *that* statement is not true. He was the exception to the rule. The way to determine the worth of a proverb, as in our example above, is to put one thousand boys in a group, give them no spiritual training at all, either at home or in the services of the church; then in another group of a thousand boys train and teach them as well as you possibly can in areas of good conduct. Out of which group will you get your law-breakers, and out of which group decent, law-abiding citizens of our country and members of the church? The spiritual training is much more important than all the other areas combined. If any has to be neglected (and most likely will not) do not neglect the spiritual. There are many ways in which a child can receive his spiritual training in the home. Here are a few:

a. Bible study in the home. I am of the firm conviction that a family should arrange a time that they can all be together and have a few moments of Bible study and prayer together. The time will have to be arranged by you. In these days of hectic living, with each member of the family on a different time schedule, your task will be a great one. But try! Read a chapter or two, have different members of the family read, and then pray. If you will set this period of time and *stick with it* from the time the child can remember, there will come a time you will be glad you did. Because David said, "Blessed (happy) is the man that walketh not in the counsel of the wicked, nor standeth in the way of sinners, nor sitteth in the seat of scoffers; but his delight is in the law of Jehovah; and on his law doth he meditate day and night" (Psalms 1:1,2).

b. Have an interest in his Bible class lessons. Insist upon his proper preparation of them. There is no greater frustration for a teacher than to have her class meet with absolutely no previous preparation, no interest in what is

67

being said, and no desire to learn. Much of this lack of interest can be avoided by you, the parent, if you see to it that your child studies his lesson before coming to the class. Do you know that we have very little interest in the things we know nothing about? And that the more we know about a subject, the more interested we get in it? If somebody begins to tell me about how a television set works, my interest span is very short. I could care less. All I want to know is, "Does it work?" I really never expect to learn about television because I have no interest in knowing. Now, if it became important that I learn about it, and I could become convinced that I should, then I know my interest would increase in the subject. And the more I learned about it, the more interested I would be in it. Well, it is of the utmost importance that we know what God has to say to us. So we should train our children in such a way that they will want to know more and more. In the sermon on the mount, Jesus said, "Blessed are they that hunger and thirst after righteousness; for they shall be filled" (Matthew 5:6). That simply means really *wanting* to know what is in God's word.

c. Never miss an opportunity to teach honesty, integrity or any moral principle from everyday incidents in the life of your child. These little things come up often. If mother is there to show the child the right way then he knows the difference between right and wrong. Suppose your child is with you at the grocery check-out counter. You give the checker a ten-dollar bill, and she gives you change for a twenty. The child is watching, and knows what is going on. But you say to the checker, "I believe I gave you a ten-dollar bill, not a twenty. You gave me too much change." What have you taught your child? Of course we know that a christian must do what is right, even though the child may not be present. But if he is, and you do what is right, it teaches him a great lesson in honesty.

d. By being the right kind of example, the kind of person you would want your child to be, you are in a better position to advise. It would be hard for a child to see the value of your advice if you were doing that thing yourself. Some of the following things we will mention fall into the category of wrong-doing, and some into the category of judgment. But with each of them, ask yourself this question: *Would I want my child to do this?* If the answer is no, you had better leave it off.

Do you smoke? Everyone agrees, especially the smoker, that it is a bad habit. It is expensive, detrimental to health, and a habit that brings reproach upon a christian. Do you want your child to smoke? Wouldn't common sense alone dictate that you break yourself of this odious habit?

How about being continually late for services, or for any other appointment? Do you think this is a good habit? You teach your child that your appointment is not important, that it really does not matter if you keep your word or not. It teaches him that disturbing worshippers who have already assembled is of no consequence. The child could get the idea from your actions that the singing is a sort of bell to get us ready for the main event.

What about telling "white lies?" Are there really any small lies? When a salesman comes to the door and you send your child to tell him you are in the shower, when the child knows you are not, what do you think you teach him?

Do you make excuses for not getting around to jobs you could do? For being lazy? For putting off important tasks? The child is learning from you to do the same thing.

Then there's the matter of attending only one service per week. A child has enough difficulty learning to do what is right without your giving him a license to do wrong. When he is grown and is on his own, what decision do you think he will make about attending services? I'll tell you what I think. I think you will be fortunate if he attends even once a week.

What do you teach your child about giving? Giving of our means is one of God's commandments. We are to give generously, cheerfully, out of our prosperity, and we are to give regularly. Jews were commanded to give a tenth, and that grew to about one-third when their government had to be supported out of their giving, also. We have no such commandment as to a stipulated amount. I am of the opinion that our giving should be far above theirs. Why not? We have a better sacrifice! We have the blood of Christ rather than the

69

blood of bulls and goats. Then let us give ourselves as a living sacrifice to him. If we slip $5.00 into the church contribution basket, when we should be giving $40.00, and our child knows what we give week after week, there will come a time when he will find out how stingy you have been with your money. Either he will follow your example, or despise your stinginess.

We could list many other things in which we set an example for our children, but these will be sufficient in showing you that it is important to set the right example.

I ran across this article on the training of children from an unknown author. I think it says so well the things I would like to say concerning the spiritual and moral training of our children that I would like to include it in this work.

### What We Give Our Children

There is a sentence from an unnamed source which says, "We have been so anxious to give our children what we didn't have that we neglected to give them what we did have."

This brings many questions to mind. What is it that children — young people — really need? What do they really want? They need love, confidence, encouragement, someone to talk to, someone to listen, standards, guidelines, laws to live by. They do not want to be left footloose in life.

They need upright examples, leaders, the faith and assurance of responsible people. They need to know that God lives, that there is a future forever, that there are rules of happiness, causes and consequences, that God's laws are still in force, and that the body and mind are sacred gifts of God — the most marvelous on earth — and that it is utter stupidity to do anything or use anything that would impair the clear, clean functioning of the body and mind and spirit of man.

Young people need to be accountable to responsible parents — to responsible people who expect much of them, and made to understand that for every infraction they (as all of us) will be called to account — that there is no way to by-pass the laws of life. They need leaders they can safely follow, leaders with moral standards and convictions, who don't fumble along with a looseness and permissiveness that can only lead to the tragedies of life.

Parents who wisely love their children will help them early to learn these lessons of life. Oh, let us give our children what we *do* have! Let us give them *ourselves, a righteous example, work to do, a sense of responsibility, a reason for facing facts, a witness of the everlasting things of life* — so that it cannot be said, "We have been so anxious to give our children what we didn't have that we neglected to give them what we did have."

I also found a fine article entitled, "Twelve Rules for Raising Delinquent Children."

1. Begin at infancy to give the child everything he wants. In this way he will grow up to believe the world owes him a living.

2. When he picks up bad words, laugh at him. He will think he is cute.

3. Never give him any spiritual training. Wait until he is twenty-one and then let him "decide for himself."

4. Avoid the use of the word "wrong." It may develop a guilt complex. This will condition him to believe later, when he is arrested for stealing a car, that society is against him and he is being persecuted.

5. Pick up everything he leaves lying around — books, clothes, shoes. Do everything for him so that he will be experienced in throwing all responsibility to others.

6. Let him read any printed matter he can get his hands on. Be careful that the silverware and drinking glasses are sterilized but let his mind feast on garbage.

7. Quarrel frequently in the presence of your children. In this way they will not be too shocked when the home is broken up later.

8. Give a child all the spending money he wants. Never let him earn his own. Why should he have things as tough as you had them?

9. Satisfy his every craving for food, drink and comfort. See that sensual desire is gratified. Denial may lead to harmful frustration.

10. Take his part against neighbors, teachers and policemen. They are all prejudiced against your child.

11. When he gets into real trouble, apologize for yourself by saying, "I never could do anything with him."

12. Prepare for a life of grief. You will be likely to have it.

## Questions On
## LESSON NO. 6

1. In what way can a mother train children so that they would become an asset to our country?

2. What has been the history of nations that have for saken and forgotten God?

3. What is the greatest thing for which parents can train their children?

4. Name some of the women of the Bible who were dedicated to rearing their children properly for service to God. Talk about each.

5. Give us an example of a very wicked woman. What did she do?

6. What is the first thing a woman should be prepared to give in order to be a good mother?

7. How do you decide what is the best division of your time?

8. Should you neglect your own spiritual life for that of your family? Give us an example of someone who did not.

9. Where do we find, "Train up a child in the way he should go, and when he is old he will not depart from it?" What does this proverb teach?

10. Give some examples of methods of training spiritually.

11. Talk about family Bible reading and prayer.

12. Discuss the importance of example-setting in:
    a. Honesty
    b. Smoking

c. Late for services habitually
d. Telling lies
e. Making excuses
f. Attending only one service per week
g. Giving

13. In the article, "What We Give Our Children," what is it that young people really need?

14. Do we have those gifts to give, regardless of our financial standing?

15. How is the best way to raise a delinquent child?

# "To Love Their Children"

So far in the second chapter of our series we have studied the necessity of a mother's allotment of the necessary time in order to train her children; the evaluation of what is important, and the greatest training of all, the child's spiritual training. But there are other areas in which children need training, and we will deal a little more briefly with these.

*4. The Child's Physical and Mental Training.* That your child needs physical and mental training in this competitive world goes without saying. They are both important. Our schools not only provide much of the mental training, but also much in the way of physical training. Of course christians know that neither of these is as important as the spiritual and moral training we give our children. Paul told Timothy, "For bodily exercise is profitable for a little; but godliness is profitable for all things, having a promise of the life which now is, and of that which is to come" (1 Timothy 4:8).

Outside the school most normal children get their fair share of exercise. They play physical games, run, jump, ride bicycles and skates, use skate-boards, they surf, swim, do exercises to build up muscles, they lift weights, play ball, and some can even be found mowing the lawn, weeding, or some such similar activity.

I think it is unprofitable in this study to spend a great deal of time on this phase of a child's development. His physical and mental training almost take care of themselves. Early in life we begin preparing him for higher education, and our hope and dream is that he will have the advantage of all the education we can give him in order to better prepare himself for a good job in this life. Since the world stresses this to the virtual exclusion of spiritual training, let us, the christians, seek to stress this the most. No child, properly trained, should be allowed to think that his mental and physical training can take precedence over his spiritual training. From his babyhood the child must be taught, and it should be stressed, that the most important thing in this life is learning what God wants us to do, and then doing it. Learning — and then making application of that learning. The world will see that he gets other training.

5. *The Child's Need for Responsibility.* "It is good for a man that he bear the yoke in his youth" (Lamentations 3:27). Remember: "God knows our frame." He said it was *good* for the youth to have responsibility and to work. It will benefit him, and bring him happiness. Now we know that a child, not having the judgment that comes with maturity, cannot see this clearly. *He* thinks he would be happiest if he had *no* responsibility, *no* work to do, and if his life could be filled with doing only what *he* would like to do. So this false concept must be untaught and the right idea made a part of his training. Whether he likes it or not a child should be taught to work around the home. When very young he can pick up his toys. A mother should be diligent in seeing that he does. A young mother once told me, "The reason most women don't follow through when they tell their child to do something is that it takes too much time and patience." Haven't you many times heard a mother tell her child to pick up a toy, then go back to her chit-chat, or television, or whatever while the child paid not the slightest attention to what she had said. Just such lack of diligence will cause that child to think it is not important to obey.

After a child is a little older he can be given jobs with more responsibility. He can earn a little spending money for himself. This will give you another realm in which you can teach your child responsibility, that of earning, saving, spending wisely and giving a portion of it to the Lord. I once knew a little girl who had 35¢ per week allowance and all on her own gave 15¢ of it to the church. Somehow those parents had impressed on her the necessity of giving as prospered.

Girls can early be taught dish-washing, making beds, sewing, shopping, cooking, etc. This will be hard and trying times for the mother. What a sloppy job they will do at first! But most of them love it and are always underfoot anyway, wanting to try their hand at anything. Give them simple little things to do at first, such as helping you make the bed or bringing silverware off the table. They will acquire more skill as they learn to do. One father I know, whom most of you know, too, was a master at good child training. From the time his oldest son could follow him about in the yard, that father had him helping. At first it was very little help to the father but bit by bit he learned a little more about it. In two or three years that boy could be left in the garden to irrigate as well as his father could. He loved it and the father had a real helper in his work. And this is to say nothing of the good accomplished by teaching that boy responsibility. Today he is a diligent worker, a fine father himself, and a faithful member of the church.

*6. The Child's Need for Understanding.* Paul said, "And, ye fathers, provoke not your children to wrath: but nurture them in the chastening and admonition of the Lord" (Ephesians 6:4). A child can be discouraged by a parent who does not understand his needs. Children are not adults, but their training must prepare them for that. Some mothers are so particular that they will not allow their daughters to do anything around the house, knowing it will not be done to perfection. But we learn by doing. How else is that child going to be ready to assume his or her role in life, either as a husband or as a wife, or a citizen, unless he has learned while a child at his parents' knees? Try to understand him, think about his problems, take time to talk to him, and above all give him the benefit of seeing that you care enough about him to want him, imperfections and all! You can either tear him down or build him up. You can destroy his confidence, or you can give him confidence. If you are so everlastingly

76

critical of everything he does, finally he will learn not to tell you everything he does or thinks. You will have built a wall between you and him and that wall will exist throughout life. More than that it will cause him to suffer a bad inferiority complex, and he will face the critical world unprepared.

Children differ in temperament just as grown people do. Some tell their parents everything they do and think. Others are more reticent. But if you have one who wants to tell you things, *LISTEN!* He wants someone to talk to and he will find someone. It had better be YOU.

*7. The Child's Need for Love.* I like that bumper sticker that says, "Have you hugged your kid today?" Be affectionate toward your child. The degree of affection will differ with every parent and with every child. Some children just will not tolerate a hug and a kiss. Others eat it up. But parents are that way, too. Sometimes children have to grow up before they learn that their parents really do love them but were unable to show it. Who knows, they may have got it from *their* parents. I had a mother like that. She would never grab me and give me a hug, but after I was grown she *loved* it if I would give her a big hug. She never paid me a compliment to my face. But she would tell others and they would tell me. I didn't know until many years later that she probably would have given anything to have been of a different disposition. You know, it doesn't take much practice. Just DO it. When it becomes necessary to discipline a child, make sure that you cause him to understand the reason for the discipline is your love. Take time to kiss and hug him after the discipline has had its effect.

*8. The Child's Need for Discipline.* Of all the admonitions given to parents in the proper training of their children, more is said about discipline than any other. Read carefully the following texts: Ephesians 6:1; Colossians 3:20; Deuteronomy 6:1-15; 1 Samuel 3:12,13; Proverbs 13:24; 19:18; 22:15; 29:17; Genesis 18:19.

Discipline will bring about self-control (Daniel 1:8; Proverbs 16:32; 25:28; Ecclesiastes 7:9).

Discipline will bring about obedience to parents (Colossians 3:20).

Discipline will cause a child to honor his parents, and care for them in old age (1 Timothy 5:4; Leviticus 19:32).

Discipline will keep a child out of trouble with those in authority, and cause him to obey the laws of the land (Romans 13:1-6).

Finally, discipline will cause him to obey God (Acts 5:29; 2 Timothy 1:5).

In order to properly discipline a child a mother has certain requirements to meet:

a. *Realize that your child is "walking in your footsteps," so do not be a problem yourself.* I think one of the best commercials I have ever seen on television was that of a father and his little son. The father was washing the car, while the son was trying his best to do everything the father did. Then the two of them went for a walk in the woods. The father sat down under a tree and the boy sat down just like he did, leaning back against the trunk. The father crossed his legs and the boy crossed his. Finally the father took a package of cigarettes out of his pocket and lighted one, tossing the package on the ground. The last thing shown was a picture of the little boy looking up at his dad and reaching out toward that package. A graphic picture it was indeed of "walking in his dad's footsteps."

b. *Be sure that what you say to your child and what you do harmonize.* Children are bright; they soon catch on. And they have a very good sense of fair play. It is not fair to tell a child to do something you yourself do not do.

c. *Remember that your child is just a child.* Each child has his own growth pattern. You cannot push growth; it must come naturally. You can easily tell when the child is ready for something. Many beautiful young girls have been ruined by mothers who pushed them into dating prematurely. They were not mature enough to handle the responsibility and the problems that come with dating. Just give them time to grow. Like a tree, it will come about naturally, beautifully, and usually sooner than you wish.

d. *You need to recognize that your child's actions cannot surpass his ability to act.* "For when by reason of the time ye ought to be teachers, ye have need again that some-

78

one teach you the rudiments of the first principles of the oracles of God: and are become such as have need of milk, and not of solid food. For everyone that partaketh of milk is without experience of the word of righteousness; for he is a babe. But solid food is for fullgrown men, even those who by reason of use have had their senses exercised to discern good and evil" (Hebrews 5:12-14). Though these members of the church should have grown, for some reason they did not. For that reason they were not able to be teachers, but had need that someone teach them. A child who is not yet ready for responsible actions should not be put into the position of acting in that capacity. That would be a catastrophe. And yet we have seen this happen when children had responsibilities thrust upon them before maturing into that task.

   e. *You need to fill your mind with good things.* Think on things that are true, honorable, just, pure, lovely and of good report, because if there is to be any virtue and praise, you will need to think on these things (Philippians 4:8). When you have *your* mind prepared you can better teach your child to prepare his mind.

   f. *Trust in God.* Yes, mother, in order to better discipline your child you need to trust in God and evaluate all that you do. Do you have in mind the things of the greatest import? If your heart is not set on spiritual things how can you impart those things to your child? Oh, we need to examine ourselves, mothers, and come to maturity ourselves before expecting to bring a child to maturity.

   g. *Work and pray for wisdom.* Finally, in preparing yourself, work and pray for wisdom. James says, "If any of you lacketh wisdom, let him ask of God, who giveth to all liberally, and upbraideth not: and it shall be given him" (James 1:5). I think the rearing of children requires the greatest amount of wisdom of any responsibility we face in life. Pray everyday about it. Ask God to continually guide you through life to the end that your child will be properly reared by you.

   *9. The Child Needs Someone He Can Depend Upon.* Here is something that happens every day in thousands of homes the world over: your child comes home from school, into the house, calls "Mother!" and when you answer he turns right around and goes out to play. Why does he do this? Because it gives him a feeling of security to know you are there. Sometimes he does not go back outside, either. Something has come up at school or on the school grounds that requires an answer for him right then. If you are there he will talk to you. If you are not, two hours later may be too late. He either forgets it or decides not to ask. When children have a question or a thought that to them is a serious one they want someone there in whom they have confidence to answer it for them. What an opportunity for the mother to instruct in ways of righteousness! If the child comes home to an empty house, or even to a sitter, there is a void. Of course, children learn to adjust, and some even do it successfully. I have known children of working mothers who have grown up to be wonderful children, fine men and women. Some mothers, because of death or illness, have been forced to work and support their family. In cases like this she hopes and prays that her children will do well on their own. But these cases are the exception to the rule. Children need someone to say "no" at times. Many times their friends are asking them to participate in something that the child knows is wrong. But peer pressure would cause him to yield if mother weren't there to say no. This takes the responsibility off him and he avoids trouble. Your child might tell you he would like to make his own decisions but in reality, especially up to a certain age, they want someone there as a shield.

10. *Clothes.* Here is a realm in which the mother is in her best role. She has the responsibility not only to select the child's wardrobe, but she can plan, sew, explain to the child why certain clothes are proper and thereby teach some wonderful lessons on modesty. There comes a time when a child should be able to select his or her own clothes. With good training over the years he will have a much better idea of what is right for him (her). Mothers, steer away from immodest clothing; too tight, too short, too whatever. Of course, your child is going to want to look just like all the others but must be taught modesty, and each mother must make her own decisions about modesty. It is interesting to

note that "modesty" is taught in the Bible without setting the exact length in inches below or above the knee. That is just one more reason we know the Bible came from God and not man. He wrote it for all generations regardless of the prevailing styles and trends. Ladies, I give you credit for knowing what is modest. Just remember that is what God requires.

11. *Entertainment.* What shall I let my child do in the way of recreation? They need it, they want it, and they are going to have it. This is a big field. Recreation is big business and the business world is working hard to get your child interested in what it has to offer in the way of entertainment or recreation. No one can make the specific choices for you. You must make them for yourselves, being guided by this one over-all principle: Any recreation or entertainment that conflicts with God's teaching for wholesomeness and purity would be unacceptable. The Bible does not deal with specifics in this field either, so we must be guided by general principles. God did say, "Keep thy heart with all diligence; for out of it are the issues of life" (Proverbs 4:23). If the entertainment does not conflict with your child's duties as a christian, or as a person who will one day be a christian, if it does not conflict with his education by taking too much time from his studies, if it does not corrupt his young, fertile mind by suggestive thoughts then, generally speaking, that entertainment would be all right. What about movies? television? books? Here again you must be the one to decide. But you *should* decide and not leave it up to the child. Be selective. Don't hesitate to turn it off, or turn him down, if it violates what you think is good. By the way, if it isn't fit for the child, it isn't fit for the adult either.

12. *Children Need to be Taught Concern for Others.* Paul has something to say on the subject of a child's concern for his parents, "Children obey your parents in the Lord: for this is right. Honor thy father and mother (which is the first commandment with promise), that it may be well with thee, and thou mayest live long on the earth" (Ephesians 6:1-3). To properly honor parents and others children need to be taught that they have an obligation to their parents to provide

81

for them in their old age, when they can no longer care for themselves. It means to be kind to all aged people. It means to respect years of wisdom, to be considerate of their weaknesses and frailties, to be willing to make concessions for grandparents and others. Common courtesy can be taught your child and should be. Paul again says, "But if any widow hath children or grandchildren, let them learn first to show piety towards their own family, and to requite their parents: for this is acceptable in the sight of God" (1 Timothy 5:4).

*13. Children Need to be Taught Hospitality.* All christians need to know and practice hospitality, so it is something children must be taught. They need to have a home, provided by you, in which their friends can gather and feel welcome. They need to know that when they are invited into other's homes they then have an obligation to return that hospitality. You can help in this teaching by suggesting. Sometimes you might be tempted to think it would be easier if you just let them go to the neighbor's house, so that your house wouldn't get messed up. Why is it that some homes always seem to be the gathering place for the children of the neighborhood, and to other places they do not go? It may be because they feel welcome at one and do not feel welcome at the other. Be sure yours is one of the homes in which they feel welcome. What memories your child will have if those memories are centered around the home and the good times he had as a youngster in that home.

*14. Children Need to be With the Right Crowd.* Part of your responsibility as a mother is to know the kind of children with whom your child is spending his time. What do they do for recreation? Where do they go? What kind of children are they? What kind of language do they use? This is another reason you need to have them in your home often. You can readily discern the kind of children they are by observing and hearing them. As children get older and go out in the evening for some of their entertainment, be sure you know where they are and where they are going. Paul said, "Be not deceived: Evil companionships corrupt good morals" (1 Corinthians 15:33). This is true for adults as well. Be not deceived just means, in our parlance, don't kid yourselves. If the child runs with the wrong crowd he will be corrupted. It is inevitable. I saw this demonstrated by a Bible class teacher. She took a handful of clean, white wooden matches. She struck one, let it burn down, then rubbed it with the clean ones between her hands. When she opened her hands all the matches were black. Again, Paul said, "Know ye not that a little leaven leaveneth the whole lump?" (1 Corinthians 5:6). If you want to reap the bitter dregs of seeing your child fall into sin just let him run with the wrong crowd long enough, or refrain from saying "no" to him. He is young and immature and sorely needs your counsel. Give it to him while there is hope.

## Questions On
## LESSON NO. 7

1. How would you compare a child's need for physical and mental training with that of his spiritual training? In what respects do they differ? Quote scripture that teaches this.

2. Name some of the ways a child can be taught responsibility. Will having responsibility hurt him or will it do him good? Since God knows our frame, what did He say in Lamentations 3:27 about bearing the yoke?

3. What would a lack of understanding on the part of the parents bring about within the child? How do we *learn* to be understanding of their needs?

4. Is it possible to withhold love from your child? Why does he need love?

5. Name some of the things proper discipline will bring about in a child. Is the Bible teaching on this subject well covered? Give some references.

6. Discuss some of the ways a mother can prepare herself in order to properly discipline the child.

7. Discuss a child's dependence upon the parents. Why is it that he is dependent upon you? How can a mother profit from this need of the child?

8. Whose responsibility is it to properly clothe a child? What underlying principle should be taught the child in clothes selection?

9. Tell me what you have learned in this lesson concerning a child's proper entertainment and recreation.

10. Why should a child be taught concern for others? How

should children requite their parents and grandparents? What does it mean to "honor?"

11. Is showing hospitality a trait that can be learned by a child? Should it? How do you go about teaching him to show hospitality?

12. Discuss the perils of evil companionships. Quote passages that teach against it. Tell how you, as a mother, can help your child avoid the pitfalls.

# Chapter Three    Lesson 8

# "To be
# Sober-Minded"

When we use the expression "sober-minded" it often conjures up a picture of a sour-faced old woman, crabby, who can never see the fun in anything and who constantly goes about with a frown on her face. This is certainly *not* the definition of "sober-minded" that is given in the word of God. There are too many passages that teach otherwise and we know the word of God is not self-contradictory. Passages such as: "A glad heart maketh a cheerful countenance; but by sorrow of heart the spirit is broken" (Proverbs 15:13). "Pleasant words are as a honeycomb. Sweet to the soul, and health to the bones" (Proverbs 16:24). "A cheerful heart is a good medicine; but a broken spirit drieth up the bones" (Proverbs 17:22). Added to these, the beatitudes in Matthew 5, in which Jesus said over and over again, "Blessed (happy) is the man . . ." God wants a christian to be cheerful; and who has a better right to be than the person who has decided to follow Christ and do that which is right? We should be happy, radiantly happy. In this respect we should be a great example to the world.

Using this lesson to teach on "happiness" does not indicate that we have forgotten our subject of "sober-minded." But to properly study the subject we should like to stress the fact that you can be sober-minded and still be "radiantly happy" provided you know the true meaning of happiness.

86

True happiness is a commendable goal in life if we properly understand the word happiness. We can better arrive at the true meaning of it if we can first determine some of the mistaken ideas people have as to what happiness is. Happiness is *NOT:*

*a. Momentary pleasure.* Moses knew that and it was recorded of him, "By faith Moses, when he was grown up, refused to be called the son of Pharaoah's daughter; choosing rather to share ill treatment with the people of God, than to *enjoy the pleasures of sin for a season . . ."* (Hebrews 11).

*b. Getting everything you want.* No, this is a self-centered attitude toward life, wanting "things" to consume on yourself. We can see too many examples of those who have material possessions in this life, but who are the most miserable creatures on this earth. Suicide rates are high among those who have lots of material possessions. Wealth does not bring happiness. A person with a craving for these things is unhappy both before and after he gets them. That is because his unhappiness or happiness is not bound up in the things themselves, but in his own inner being. It is an attitude toward life. As we have stressed before, attitude plays such a big role in our living a christian life. Let us get our attitudes straight and other things will take care of themselves.

*c. Something you can corner and can't lose.* No, on the contrary, happiness is very fleeting and elusive. You think you just about have it in your grasp and it is gone again. Children think if they just can get that bicycle, that doll, that whatever, they will be happy. Give it to them and fifteen minutes later they want something else.

But, then, how does happiness come and what is it? People who are happy are better off physically, mentally, and spiritually. That is the whole of life. They make better students, better wives and mothers, and better members of the church. And because happiness is difficult to contain in one person, it rubs off on those with whom we come in contact, thereby sweetening and enriching the lives of everyone around us. What an influence for good a truly happy christian is!

Happiness cannot be pursued and caught, as one would catch a beautiful butterfly. The expression, "Happiness is a by-product of service" is not just a trite saying. It has its roots in fundamental truths. Jesus said, "He that findeth his life shall lose it; and he that loseth his life for my sake shall find it" (Matthew 10:39). The meaning of this verse is aptly portrayed by the story of the young boy immersed in a game of baseball. He knew his mother had told him to be at home at a certain time but he became so absorbed in doing what he loved to do that time had no meaning for him. When thus absorbed he is playing the best game of ball possible for him. He is supremely happy. That's the way it is with living the christian life. When we are totally committed and absorbed in doing what Christ commanded us we lose ourselves in respect of other things. We lose our own selfish desires and ambitions. We lose our fear of talking to other people about Christ; we lose interest in material things of life; they mean nothing to us. It is at these times that we give our best service to Christ, and it is in this way that we gain happiness. When completely absorbed in doing for others, with little thought as to our own welfare, we derive the greatest amount of happiness possible for us. Have you ever experienced the feeling of giving someone you love a gift, something you knew that person really wanted? Perhaps you sacrificed a great deal to get it for him or her. But didn't you derive a great happiness in the giving? Didn't it make you happier to give that gift than to receive one? It is quite an experience; because true happiness is quite an experience.

Now considering the fact that "God knows our frame" and knowing that he wants us to be happy, would common sense dictate that if we, as women, fulfill the role God has set for us we would gain the deepest happiness possible? I think this makes sense.

In Proverbs 31 we read about a worthy woman and we see what she did to attain that status.

a. She gained the trust and confidence of her husband.
b. She did him good all the days of her life.
c. She worked willingly with her hands.
d. She rose up early and gave food to her household.
e. She considered a field and bought it.
f. She girded her loins with strength and made strong

88

her arms.

g. She made and sold garments.

h. She helped the poor and needy.

i. She was the means of seeing that her husband was respected.

j. She developed strength and dignity.

k. She had no fear of the future.

l. She opened her mouth with wisdom and kindness.

m. She looked well to the ways of her house, and was not lazy.

n. She was praised by her children and her husband.

Truly it could be said of this woman, "Many daughters have done worthily, but thou excellest them all. Grace is deceitful, and beauty is vain, but a woman that feareth Jehovah, she shall be praised. Give her of the fruit of her hands; and let her works praise her in the gates" (Proverbs 31:29-31).

What better example could we use in this study of women and their training than this given in the Proverbs? This example is inspired of God. If we carefully study and follow each of these principles of her life we will have successfully learned what our role is, what true happiness is, and will attain not only the love, respect, and praise of our husbands here on this earth, but will attain Heaven itself. These are profitable goals; work for them. Every woman should seek to attain them.

In going about to attain these goals let us pay some attention to each of the things mentioned about the worthy woman in Proverbs and perhaps we can better arrive at our goals.

*a. She Gained the Trust and Confidence of her Husband:*

"The heart of her husband trusteth in her, and he shall have no lack of gain" (Verse 11). Sad though it may be, there are many husbands in this world who cannot trust their wives. The wives are busily engaged in flirtations, outside love affairs, drinking, gambling, and too many other activities in which no one should indulge. Wives, do not give your husbands any reason to suspect you are interested in another man. You may think this cannot happen if two people are members of the church, and it shouldn't. But we know of too many cases where it has. I know preachers whose wives have not only had flirtations but actually have had love affairs with other men. Consider: how does this come about? How could a christian let things get out of hand? Mostly because of seemingly innocent incidents. Two couples go out together often, are thrown into close relationships, one wife becomes too intimate with the other man or vice versa. Then a closer relationship begins and finally the ultimate act of betrayal. It can happen. It has happened many times. Before it does with you take the warning from these lessons. Do not put yourself into any kind of compromising situation where you or the man may be tempted. You may not resist the temptation.

Again, your husband's lack of confidence can come about through your misuse and handling of money. You may spend him into the poorhouse, and he may be compelled to take over the money management himself.

Or, sadly enough, there are many alcoholics among women who are alone most of the day with time on their hands. They fall into little traps such as taking a little drink for "medicinal purposes" or pills to get over a bad case of depression. Anything that could be habit-forming should be avoided at all times. If necessity causes a doctor to prescribe such, be very careful. Take for as short a time as possible, so that you do not become dependent on such for sustenance.

Here is another avenue in which women mismanage money: they become race-track addicts. Their gambling becomes a craze with them. Phone calls to their bookies are made from their homes, and there goes the husband's paycheck down the drain. It soon gets to the point that the paycheck is not enough and she begins to sell off household items that will bring in a little money. What a sad state of affairs. No wonder the heart of her husband can't trust in her.

Instead of any of these, if a woman diligently applies herself to the role of homemaking, properly handles money, scrupulously keeps her integrity and morals, conducts herself as a christian should in everything, then her husband has no fear of her conduct, has no fear that when he is away from home things will go wrong, and then it can safely be said that he can trust her.

   *b. Did Him Good all the Days of her Life:*

   "She doeth him good and not evil all the days of her life" (Verse 12). Everything that you can do in the role God has assigned you will do your husband good. If you are a good housekeeper, if you are happy and pleasant to be around, if you are honest, industrious, highly moral and kind, this is all to be included in the things it takes to "do him good, and not evil."

   *c. Worked Willingly With Her Hands:*

   "She seeketh wool and flax, and worketh willingly with her hands" (Verse 13). The footnote on "willingly" is "at the business of." She is busily engaged in industrious habits. She *sought* wool and flax, and was busily engaged in the business of making something of it. Remember that in those days women not only made their garments, they made the material that made the garments. And not only the material but the thread itself was spun by them. It was quite a chore to be responsible for the making of the garments for her household. No wonder she had to arise so early in the morning! In our modern society we have no idea of all the things a woman had to do to be a good wife and mother. But we are delighted that we do not have to know. I rather like it like it is! In spite of our modern conveniences we can still be classified as a "worthy woman" if we will be busily engaged in the pressing duties of our own households. Notice, too, that she not only worked with her hands, but worked *willingly*. There is a vast difference, and when we get ourselves into the frame of mind of doing it *willingly* then it can truthfully be said that we have learned the true secret of happiness.

   *d. Rose Up Early and Gave Food to her Household:*

   A few lessons back we talked about preparing breakfast for the family. Teachers in public schools say that they can instantly tell the students that have been up long enough to have had a good breakfast. They are brighter, more alert, and their capacity for learning is much greater. I am sure it would be the same for the husband on the job. This virtuous woman "riseth up also while it is yet night, and giveth food to her household, and their tasks to her maidens" (Verse 15). They assigned the servants their jobs for the day. She was evidently a woman of means and could afford servants. This is no sin if it does not deprive you of your duties. She worked hard all day long for her household right along with the servants. Her husband and children were fed their breakfast. Do not let your opportunities for true happiness flee because of some selfish motive.

   e. *Considered a Field and Bought It:*

"She considereth a field, and buyeth it; with the fruit of her hands she planteth a vineyard" (Verse 16). This woman was no dimwit. She had the intelligence to look over a field, decide if it was a good buy, and buy it. Her husband trusted her to make decisions like this. Then she planted a vineyard with her own hands. She had an eye to the future proceeds of this vineyard and thought she could make some money for the family. You are not limited to household chores in being a good wife and mother. Can you see some way, without neglecting home duties that you can add to the family income? This is not only not sinful, it is following the example of a worthy woman. Do it!

   f. *Girded her Loins with Strength and made Strong her Arms:*

I do not get the idea that this was purely physical strength, though I think of necessity it included that. The woman "girdeth her loins with strength, and maketh strong her arms" (Verse 17). In other passages we have such teaching as, "Stand there, having girded your loins with truth . . ." (Ephesians 6:14). We can "gird ourselves with humility" (1 Peter 5:5). I think the real meaning of "girding oneself with strength" would be to "clothe" oneself with strength or humility. We should become determined in our minds to do God's will, and have the fortitude to stay with it. If we have a tendency to "slack off" that would be the very opposite of a determined spirit. This woman "made up her mind" what she was going to do, and did it.

   g. *Made and Sold Garments:*

"She perceiveth that her merchandise is profitable; her lamp goeth not out by night" (Verse 18). "She maketh linen garments and selleth them, and delivereth girdles unto the merchant" (Verse 24). She was a business woman. The work was performed in her home, but the selling of her merchandise took her into the market places of the merchants. She neglected not the home over which she reigned as queen, but she diligently pursued other things as well, and was praised for it.

*h. Helped the Poor and Needy:*

"She stretcheth out her hand to the poor; yea, she reacheth forth her hands to the needy" (Verse 20).

What a gracious quality in a worthy woman! Here is a person that was industrious, knowledgeable, thrifty, virtuous, one who had material possessions but who at the same time was touched with the feelings of those in need. It is a quality of tenderness and love that should be emulated by all of us who seek to be worthy women. It should be part of our sober thinking, because it is stressed in God's word and causes us to have that happiness we desire.

Our helping those in need goes beyond mere necessities of physical comforts. We should train ourselves to notice people. Really take time to look beyond one's little shell. There are so many needs that we can provide. A teen-ager is having problems; a child is in tears; a woman is on the verge of a break-down — do we care enough? When a person wants to talk are we ready to listen? Learn to catch the little word or glance that tells you somebody is reaching out for help. There are many ways this becomes apparent if we will practice the art of "hearing."

As far as helping those in need of material things is concerned, I know that all of us sympathize with people who are in dire need, and will give willingly to alleviate their suffering. It is not often nowadays, in our affluent society, that these needs arise. But as we go through life, let us attune our ears to hear the cries for help from those with whom we come in contact.

*i. Was the Means of Seeing that her Husband Was Respected:*

"Her husband is known in the gates, when he sitteth among the elders of the land" (Verse 23). I know very little about the customs of those days, but from reading the book of Job and this passage, and perhaps the book of Ruth, we gain some little inkling. It seemed that men who were admired and respected by the citizens of that community had seats of prominence in some public place. Other people paid them the respect due them, and "listened when they talked." By properly fulfilling her role at home the wife had much to do with how much her husband was respected and heard. If she were the wrong kind of woman whom he could not bring into line, then he lost the respect and admiration of the other men.

Even though today we have different customs, your actions still reflect on your husband. They are judged considerably by how you perform. There are numerous instances of business firms interviewing the wife along with her husband, when they are considering him for a position with them. If the wife is asked, "Would you be willing to move to another city?" and she answers no, that man is rejected. He can have no future with that company because they know he cannot be depended upon to make the decisions. They know he is ruled by his wife's whims, and that is not safe ground for them.

Elders have this same admonition in order for them to qualify as elders. Not only elders' wives, but their children, have a great deal to do with whether a man can be qualified to serve in this capacity. If a man has to find out what his wife thinks about a certain decision in the work of that church, he is not qualified to be an elder.

Preachers' wives have much to do with whether his work is pleasing and profitable to a congregation or not. If she is not in subjection she can cause an untold amount of harm, and a preacher soon finds himself looking for another place. But if a wife fulfills her role of being in subjection to her husband, she can further him in this great work.

*j. Developed Strength and Dignity:*

"Strength and dignity are her clothing: and she laugheth at the time to come" (Verse 25).

This verse is similar to the one that talks about girding her loins with strength. Here the word "clothing" is used in about the same meaning.

A woman who has laid up sufficiently for the future has

94

no fear of poverty. Another good lesson along this line is, "Go to the ant, thou sluggard: consider her ways, and be wise: which having no chief, overseer, or ruler, provideth her bread in the summer, and gathereth her food in the harvest" (Proverbs 6:6-8). Yes, this worthy woman considered well the needs of her household and provided for those needs while the time was right.

Picture in your mind a harvest of good food, at bargain prices, in the season of fruits and vegetables. Now is the time to gather and prepare them for future use. But here is an indolent, slothful woman who will not go to the trouble to get that merchandise and put it up. She misses her opportunity. When winter comes along, when fruits and vegetables are expensive, she takes her husband's hard-earned money, goes to the store and pays exorbitant prices for those same products. How foolish! A little forethought and she could have had strawberries, pickles, squash, beans, corn, tomatoes, tomato sauce, relishes, peaches, apricots, berries, jellies and jams, all kinds of goodies. Besides being cheaper they are better. Then there is the actual fun of doing it, the good feeling of accomplishing and saving.

Even today in our affluent society one of the best ways wives can help out with the food budget is to prepare food for storage, either frozen or canned. Ask those who have tried it and they will tell you it is worth while.

*k. Opened Her Mouth with Wisdom and Kindness:*

"She openeth her mouth with wisdom; and the law of kindness is on her tongue" (Verse 26).

What a great thing to be said of anyone, that she opened her mouth with wisdom. How hard it is to make wise statements. Wisdom does not come without experience and hard study. Many foolish and hurtful things crowd into our lives, and immaturity is a breeding place for them. Maturity brings knowledge and wisdom only if a person applies herself to attain them. Pray God for wisdom (James 1:5); he said he would give it to the man who asked. But the man who asks God for wisdom needs also to do everything he is capable of doing to attain the knowledge of God. If you do what *you* can and ask God to do the rest, He has promised to help.

And then, *kindness:* a person may open his mouth with wisdom, have much knowledge, and yet be very brutal with his tongue. He is not tolerant of another person's lack of knowledge, with his immaturity or his problems. He is caustic and sharp-tongued. People will not go to that person for advice or counsel. They are afraid of his sarcasm, of being derided or cut down to size. When you talk to people be considerate of their problems, even of their deficiencies, and have kindness on your tongue.

*l. Looked Well to the Ways of her House; Was Not Lazy:*

"She looketh well to the ways of her household; and eateth not the bread of idleness" (Verse 27).

It takes effort to do all the things that need to be done around the house. But slacking off doesn't make the job easier, it makes it harder. Again, as we have stressed in past lessons, a person needs good balance in this field as in all other fields. You can become so dedicated to keeping house that you lose sight of everything else. This is too much dedication. A well-ordered house is a joy, but a well-ordered wife is a greater joy. And to be well-ordered you *need* some relaxation and time off from the job. Industry recognizes this, thus providing coffee-breaks and vacation time. Housewives need time off, some time for inner contemplation and a soothing and revitalizing of self. Take it, but don't let it become an obsession with you. Don't become lazy and indifferent toward your job at home. Good balance, remember?

*m. Was Praised by her Children and Husband:*

"Her children rise up. and call her blessed: Her husband also, and he praiseth her, saying, Many daughters have done worthily, but thou excellest them all" (Verses 28, 29).

The reward of all the industry, thrift, energy and wisdom that this worthy woman put into her work was the praise and admiration of her children and her husband. This is the greatest praise we have on this earth, to know that our husband and our children think we are "tops." If your husband thinks you are doing your part it spurs him on to do more for you. It is a sort of cycle that comes right back to you. You haven't lost by being self-sacrificing, but rather you have gained. Best of all you know you have fulfilled your role and are acceptable in God's sight. In conclusion God sums it all up like this:

"Grace is deceitful, and beauty is vain: but a woman that feareth Jehovah, she shall be praised. Give her of the fruit of her hands; and let her works praise her in the gates" (Verses 30, 31).

In the sober thoughts of our hearts, when we explore thoughtfully the inner workings of our minds, we cannot but know that in order to achieve true happiness, to be the sober-minded person God has asked us to be, we must have the qualities of this worthy woman. This would be a good plaque to mount on our mirrors and study each morning of our lives. Do we really want to be a worthy woman? Do we really want to attain sober-mindedness? Then apply these principles.

In an earlier lesson we talked at length about women working. We mentioned the reasons she should not, and the reasons she should. We also noted that under some circumstances working out was commendable. It was in the case of this worthy woman, since she was commended by the Lord.

I see no conflict in the two teachings if we understand the whys and wherefores of our working. I see a vast difference in the way this woman went about her work and the way some women work outside the home. You should note that this woman's interest was in her home, primarily, in her husband and children. Most of her activity was centered around these. Incidental to her priorities was the fact that she earned money.

Keep your interests in home, husband and children, and you could not go too far wrong in working.

## Questions On
## LESSON NO. 8

1. Does being "sober-minded" mean being unhappy and gloomy? Does God want us to be happy? Can you quote passages to prove?

2. What are the mistaken ideas people have about what happiness is?

3. What is true happiness and how does it come?

4. Can happiness be pursued and caught?

5. In our example of the worthy woman, what is the first thing she did to attain her position of a worthy woman? How did she go about doing this? Name ways in which a woman could destroy trust.

6. What is the second way in which you can attain this goal?

7. Tell how the worthy woman worked with her hands.

8. What did she do early in the morning?

9. Did she have any interests outside the home? How did they manifest themselves?

10. What does it mean to gird one's loins with strength?

11. How did this woman make money? Was this hard work? Did it lessen her responsibility toward household chores?

12. What quality of benevolence did this woman have? How can we show this same quality?

98

13. How does a woman aid in the respect shown her husband by the business world?

14. Name some ways women can laugh at the "time to come."

15. How do we learn to say wise and kind things?

16. Was this woman idle? Discuss idleness and its fruits.

17. Who were the first to praise her? What did her husband say of her?

18. Do you think it worthwhile to emulate this worthy woman? Why?

19. What did Jehovah say of her?

20. How can we harmonize this principle with that of Lesson 5 in which we stressed the idea of the husband as the provider?

# "To be Sober-Minded"

In our last lesson, under the heading "sober-minded," we studied how women can attain true happiness. We discovered that true happiness is not momentary pleasure, not getting everything we want, is not something you pursue and catch, but that true happiness comes to us by fulfilling our roles as wives and mothers in the same way the "worthy woman" of Proverbs 31 did. She fulfilled the role God gave to women in respect of her duties to husband and children, and who can deny that this woman found fulfillment in this way? At least she pleased her family and God, and what more could one want?

But since we are dealing with the portion of this scripture that admonishes the older women to teach the young to be "sober-minded," I think it behooves us to find out what this expression means and how we can go about attaining this worthy attribute.

Webster defines sober as: serious, solemn, sedate; quiet; characterized by reason, sanity, or self-control; humble; simple, not affected by passion or prejudice; well-balanced, regular, steady. The opposite meaning of sober-minded according to the best information I have of the Bible meaning of the word is: frivolous; flighty; light-minded. We know people who go through life with seldom a serious thought. Everything is one big joke to them, and they think they have been appointed head joker. It is hard to get persons of this type into a serious discussion. Their minds are not turned in this direction. They read the trashiest of literature, watch the lightest of programs on television. In order for a person to attain to sober-mindedness she should train herself by the reading of good literature. The Bible is the best, followed by articles written by christians, commentaries, a good use of a library on religious topics; then good books on worthwhile topics other than religious, good television shows (there are a few), with periods of meditation and musing with one's self to establish the habit of serious thinking. The Bible teaches us in many different places and ways that we are the product of our thinking. "For as he thinketh within himself, so is he . . ." and like passages.

a. *Serious; solemn; sedate; quiet:*

The serious person is earnest, not joking or trifling; is sincere; concerned with grave matters requiring careful consideration. This is not to say that a person could never joke, never be light-hearted, nor have a thought that was flighty. But this should not be the pattern for one's life. When the time comes for serious thinking (and hopefully those times would outweigh the other), then we should learn to give grave and serious consideration to these problems. After all, life is not a picnic ground to provide us with a life-time of frivolity and pleasure. Rather, life is a preparation for eternity, and our preparation for eternity is serious business. It requires sober thinking and presents grave problems which must be faced and with which we must deal in the wisest possible way. The Bible teaches us that our behaviour as women should be characterized by sobriety. Paul said, "In like manner that women adorn themselves in modest apparel, with shamefastness and sobriety . . ." (1 Timothy 2:9). This same quality of soberness is the topic of our lesson here. And in the same passage we read, "Let a woman learn in quietness with all subjection" (Verse 11). The quietness mentioned here is also one of the definitions given by Webster for the word sober. Paul admonished all to "study to be quiet, and to do your own business . . ." (1 Thessalonians 4:11). This definition of "quiet" would indicate taking care to tend to your own thing and not be meddling in other men's matters. The same thing is taught again, "Now them that are such (disorderly, busybodies) we command and exhort in the Lord Jesus Christ, that with quietness they work, and eat their own bread" (2 Thessalonians 3:12).

However difficult it may be to put into words we cannot help seeing the meaning of quietness is that quality characteristic of a peaceable, sober-minded individual. It gives us a picture of a humble, sedate person rather than a loud-mouthed, nagging woman.

*b. Characterized by reason, sanity or self-control:*

Here is another quality of the sober-minded person that is to be emulated by all christians, and is especially emphasized as a quality to be learned by all young women. The Bible is a *reasonable* book, with *reasonable* guide-lines for us to follow. It is a way of life that appeals to the intellect. It is with our minds that we come to a realization of what God expects of His creation. Paul said, "I beseech ye therefore brethren, by the mercies of God, to present your bodies a living sacrifice, holy, acceptable to God, which is your spiritual service" (Romans 12:1). The word "spiritual" in this verse means "belonging to the reason." God knows our frame, and having made us knows that his law will appeal to the reason.

*Sanity* simply means mental health, the quality of being able to reason, and especially in our study to reason on God's word. If you take the time in your life to really apply yourself to a study of God's revelation, it will leave little time for frivolity and lightness. This life is a training ground for eternity and requires diligent preparation.

*Self-control* is taught many places in God's word. You will not practice self-control unless you give sober reflection on the principles God has taught us. A passage that needs to be seriously studied by all of us is Peter's teaching on qualities to be added to our lives. He said we should, in order to be partakers of the divine nature, add to our faith virtue, knowledge, *self-control,* patience, godliness, brotherly kindness and love (2 Peter 1:1-11). The meaning of self-control is evident in the word itself. It simply means the control of self. We sometimes are our own worst enemies. A person who can see his faults and weaknesses and learns to control them has

102

indeed mastered the art of self-control. There are so many areas in which we need this quality. We need it in the realm of our speech, in our physical habits, in our thoughts, in our actions, and indeed in all areas of living.

Do we have the ability to control self? Well, of course! No one else can control it for us. If we do not, no one will! We see too many cases of poor remnants of humanity who have neglected this vital quality. Their minds and bodies are a mere shambles of what God would have us to be. "There hath no temptation taken you but such as man can bear: but God is faithful, who will not suffer you to be tempted above that ye are able; but will with the temptation make also the way of escape that ye may be able to endure it" (1 Corinth - ians 10:13).

God has promised us the way of escape and God's prom- ises do not fail. *Our* job is to look for the way of escape and take it. That is the point at which so many fail. They simply do not avail themselves of the way out that God provided.

If we were in a burning building and a way of escape had been provided by firemen, we would be utter fools to remain in the building and refuse to use the escape. So classify the person who refuses to use God's way of escape. This is the person who refuses to control self. You *can* say "no" to temptation.

c. *Humility* is another phase of sober-mindedness. Like other definitions, humility is a quality well-defined in God's word. I suppose the best known example of humility was taught by Jesus. The setting is in John 13, at the supper before the feast of the passover, where Jesus was eating with his disciples. He arose from the supper and began to wash the disciples' feet. Simon Peter said to him, "Lord, dost thou wash my feet?" (Verse 6). Jesus answered, "What I do thou knowest not yet; but thou shalt understand hereafter" (Verse 7). Peter knew he was washing feet. But Jesus was trying to teach them another lesson, the lesson of humility. He explained it by saying, "For I have given you an example, that ye also should do as I have done to you. Verily, verily I say unto you, a servant is not greater than his lord; neither one that is sent greater than he that sent him" (Verses 15 and

103

16). At another time Jesus taught his disciples, "Ye know that the rulers of the Gentiles lord it over them, and their great ones exercise authority over them. *Not so* shall it be among you: but whosoever would become great among you shall be your servant: even as the Son of man came not to be ministered unto but to minister, and to give his life a ransom for many" (Matthew 20:25-28). Of all people to whom mankind should bow the knee and strive to serve, Jesus would have to be acclaimed the greatest. Yet his example for us was one of service and ministry. His lesson on humility should be emulated by all of us.

True humility is not a put-on, a mere sham. It bespeaks a frame of mind free from arrogance, knowing that our own talents and virtues are far from perfect.

"The fear of Jehovah is the instruction of wisdom; and before honor goeth humility" (Proverbs 15:33).

"There are six things which Jehovah hateth, yea seven which are an abomination unto him; haughty eyes (etc. . . .)" (Proverbs 6:16-17).

"Pride goeth before destruction, and a haughty spirit before a fall" (Proverbs 16:18).

*d.* Another definition for sober-minded is: *Simple,* not affected by passion or prejudice.

Simple does not carry with it a meaning of being mentally retarded. Rather simplicity can also mean uncomplicated, not compound or complex, without addition, unadorned, without guile or deceit; innocent; without ostentation; natural; and one definition says humble, which we have already studied. These are the good ways in which the word "simple" is used.

How many times have we seen otherwise intelligent beings turned into unthinking tyrants because they were acting from prejudice or passion? This kind of action is a far cry from the sober-minded, rational person. We alone have the power to train our minds, to control our thoughts and actions It is up to each one of us to do so.

To be sober-minded then is to be the opposite of anyone who is flighty, frivolous, and light-minded. I cannot imagine a person who has assumed the responsibilities of being a christian, a wife, and a mother who would not desire to make her life conform to the kind of sober-mindedness we have studied in these lessons. I think your very desire to study these lessons attests to the fact that you want to be such. First of all because God has commanded it of us, and secondly because in so doing we will attain the true happiness we all so greatly desire.

## Questions On
## LESSON NO. 9

1. What does the Bible teach on sober-mindedness?

2. In what ways can one train herself to look upon the gravity of life, and attain to this quality of sober-mindedness?

3. What is the definition of serious?

4. Are we saying that a christian can never smile or joke?

5. Quote passages that deal with sobriety.

6. What does the Bible say about quietness? What does it mean?

7. In what way does reason, sanity and self-control enter into the picture of being sober-minded?

8. Can prejudice or passion disrupt sanity? Tell how.

9. Quote passages in which self-control is taught.

10. Can we control self? How?

11. What is true humility?

12. Who gave us the greatest example of humility? In what way?

13. Quote other passages denouncing a haughty spirit.

14. What is the proper definition of simplicity in our study of this subject?

15. What happens when a person acts from prejudice or passion?

16. Who will control your thoughts and actions?

106

# Chapter Four

# "Chaste"

Webster says the definition of chaste is: "Not indulging in unlawful sexual activity; virtuous; said especially of women. Not indecent; modest; restrained and simple in style. To be pure in life, not contaminated with filth, the opposite of that which is immoral."

The Bible definition is: "Keep thyself pure" (1 Timothy 5:22). "Blessed are the pure in heart; for they shall see God" (Matthew 5:8). Peter admonishes wives who are in subjection to their husbands to maintain the proper conduct toward them, that they may be gained by your behavior "beholding your 'chaste' behavior coupled with fear" (1 Peter 3:2). Another from Paul, "For I am jealous over you with a godly jealousy: for I espoused you to one husband, that I might present you as a pure virgin to Christ" (2 Corinthians 11:2). [The King James Version says, "that I might present you as a chaste virgin to Christ."]

More time could be spent on this one word and all it involves than on all the rest of our lessons. I suspect the discussion of it will create more questions, and involve more controversy than on any other phase of our study, probably. For herein we find the most basic of human urges, the urges that drive people to do all those immoral practices that are so foreign to God's wishes for his people.

The admonition for chastity touches the lives of every

one of us. It is not confined to one sex, it is not confined to youth, and it is not confined to christians. God's moral law is for everyone in this world. It is just as much a sin in the sight of God for a person who is not a member of the church to commit adultery as it is for a christian. Sometimes young people have the mistaken idea that they can "sow their wild oats" in their youth, then become members of the church without repenting, and that this will be acceptable in God's sight. Not so! It is true that a person can be forgiven of any sin of which he repents, but certainly he must admit guilt, and ask to be forgiven before God will do so. It is not just automatically wiped out.

Another thing about sin is the consequences of it. The harvest of "sowing wild oats" will come back to haunt and plague a person many times over. The flagrant disregard for God's moral law will lead that person into situations that a lifetime of right living cannot erase. The sin is erased, forgiven, remembered no more by God, but the consequences of that sin may be carried until death. As an illustration of this fact, suppose a person robs a bank and is caught. He goes to jail and spends ten years behind bars. His family is without a means of support and falls into dire straits. They are not being punished for his sin but suffer as a consequence of it. When he gets out of jail he finds it difficult to get employment. His sin, for which he did time, and which is eradicated as far as justice is concerned, is still lingering to haunt him. He is still reaping the harvest.

A young girl lets herself be talked into an immoral act of fornication. Afterward she is penitent, asks God's forgiveness, the forgiveness of her family, and possibly the church. But the illegitimate act has resulted in the birth of a child. A lifetime of right living from then on does not erase the harvest of one rash wrong. No matter which way she turns (and hopefully it is in the right way) the result of that sin will be with her as long as she lives. Please note that I have called the "act" illegitimate, not the "child." A student in one of my classes called my attention to a statement I had made about an "illegitimate child." She said, "It is not the child who is illegitimate." I agree and have made this correction in subse-

108

quent classes.

So I think above all other things we teach, we need the lesson on chastity. Not only in our own lives do we need this lesson, but we need to be able in turn to teach it to our children and others. Teach them early, positively and well.

In that great "sermon on the mount" given by our Lord, he said: "Blessed (Happy) are the pure in heart, for they shall see God" (Matthew 5:8). Regardless of anything this life can give us, or regardless of the things we have to give up, it will all be worth it if we can just some day "see God."

As we study this great subject keep in mind that our main purpose in life is so to live and so prepare ourselves that eventually we can "see God." It is a great reward for the very hard striving we must do while on earth to keep ourselves pure or chaste. The reward will make it easier to conduct ourselves properly here.

Other than a desire to go to Heaven there are also earthly rewards for being chaste. It gives us beauty of appearance, thus improving our looks. Indulgence in things of this world such as drinking, smoking, lewd conduct of any sort tends to the destruction of the body. Vital organs fail, or are so crippled that they function poorly. Diseases of many kinds prey upon persons who have abused their bodies with drink, dope and tobacco. For the sake of health and beauty, for serenity of mind, for inner peace and contentment, for the ability to look a person in the eye, and to present to the world an untroubled, calm countenance, living a chaste life pays off. Look into the face of a bleary-eyed wino, who has drunk deep of the dregs of sin, lying in a gutter, dirty, sick, miserable, and tell me that person is having it easy! The Bible says, "The way of the transgressor is hard" (Proverbs 13:15).

Chastity gives us strength of character, and strength of character gives us the ability to meet people, makes it easier for us to mix and mingle with the better things and people of this life and feel no shame.

Chastity gives us protection. Promiscuity gives no protection. When a man and woman enter into a marriage contract, he assumes the role of protector and provider, and feels a definite sense of loyalty to her, and responsibility for her welfare. But if a woman is promiscuous in her relationship with a man, lives with him without the protection of the marriage contract, he feels no such sense of duty toward her. He can, and does, leave such a woman at any time he desires without any feeling of responsibility. So even with nothing else (and there is much more), chastity is the better role.

Remember this simple rule for chastity as is given in God's law: No sexual relationships before marriage; no sexual relationships outside of marriage. This law was intended for all people, for all times, since the beginning of man and woman on this earth, and was given to last until this life is over. It is not a law just for parents or for grandparents. It is for you and for your children and grandchildren. It is a law created for our happiness and well-being. Think with me for a moment. How much heart-ache and unhappiness could have been avoided if this law of chastity had not been broken. What happy relationships there would be in this world! Do you not see the benefit of such a law? Then resolve now to abide by it as long as you live.

Some of the realms included in the word "chaste" should be explored. Within this word we could list:

1. Unlawful sexual relationships;
2. Indecent dress;
3. Filthy language;
4. Immodesty (other than in dress);
5. Flamboyant in actions.

These categories should be explored at length to find out what God has to say about each:

*1. Unlawful sexual relationships:*

The Bible is very explicit on this subject. God uses such plainness of speech, such fulness and clarity of expression, that no one can misunderstand his teaching. Paul writes to the Romans, making a list of the prevalent sins among the Gentiles in his day. It reads like a modern newspaper account of the happenings of our society. Under the unlawful sexual relationships the following headings should be studied:

a. Lesbianism: "Their women changed the natural use into that which is against nature" (Romans 1:26).

b. Homosexuality: "And likewise also the men, leaving the natural use of the woman, burned in their lust one toward another, men with men working unseemliness, and receiving in themselves that recompense of their error which was due" (Romans 1:27).

c. Incest: "None of you shall approach to any that are near of kin . . . father . . . mother . . . father's wife (and others)" (Leviticus 18:6,8).

d. Sodomy: "Thou shalt not lie with mankind, as with womankind: It is an abomination" (Leviticus 18:22,23). "And thou shalt not lie with any beast . . ." (Verse 23). The word sodomy itself comes from the city of Sodom, wherein lived Lot and his family, and which city God burned to the ground because of this heinous crime.

e. Adultery: "And the man that committeth adultery with another man's wife . . . the adulterer and the adulteress shall surely be put to death" (Leviticus 20:10). "Be not deceived: neither . . . adulterers . . . shall inherit the kingdom of God" (1 Corinthians 6:9).

f. Fornication: "Be not deceived: neither . . . fornicators . . . shall inherit the kingdom of God" (1 Corinthians 6:9).

These horrible sins, so plainly set forth in the word of God, can all have forgiveness. When a person repents of these God will make him as pure as a newborn baby, all filthiness washed away. "Or know ye not that the unrighteous shall not inherit the kingdom of God? Be not deceived: neither fornicators nor idolators, nor adulterers, nor effeminate, nor abusers of themselves with men, nor thieves, nor covetous, nor drunkards, nor revilers, nor extortioners, shall inherit the kingdom of God. *And such were some of you:* but ye were washed, but ye were sanctified, but ye were justified in the name of the Lord Jesus Christ, and in the Spirit of our God" (1 Corinthians 6:9-11). What a wonderful hope is held out to the sinner whose life has been blackened so dreadfully by sin! But ladies, before we kid ourselves into thinking we can commit such and then get forgiveness later on, ask yourself the question: "What benefit would I derive from doing such things? Would the gratification of these fleshly desires make me —"

1. A better wife and mother?

111

2. A better person emotionally? Many people's lives have been wrecked by emotional illness brought on by such actions.

3. A better homemaker? People wrapped up in unchaste lives seem to lose all interest in making a good home. The two are not compatible.

4. A better citizen? Contrariwise, it brings on illicit relationships that lead to illicit meetings, to an actual disregard for the laws of the land, to say nothing of the laws of the husband, or of God, or the parents. It creates a spirit of lawlessness (iniquity).

5. A better child of God? No! On the contrary, if pursued it will send your soul to hell. Your Father is the devil, not God.

6. A candidate for heaven? No, it leads toward a total disregard for things of a spiritual nature. No longer do you have a love for God or for the study of his word.

7. A help in the upbuilding of my country? If our nation ever gets to the place that the majority of its people conduct themselves with no regard for God's law, that nation will fall. It was the underlying cause of the fall of Rome, Greece, Persia, Babylonia, Sodom and Gomorrah. "The wicked shall be turned back unto Sheol, *even all the nations that forget God"* (Psalms 9:17).

What is the prevailing teaching of "The New Morality?" Just the opposite of all we have talked about in regard to chastity. We hear much about the New Morality. The advocates of this new (old) teaching are vocal about their beliefs. "Gays" are nothing new. But there was a time when they were afraid to speak out, admit they were, and defy decent people and God's laws. But something has changed all that. We have a permissive society that no longer condemns anything and these people know that the time is right to get their ideas into the law books, to promote "gays" in our public school teaching program, in civil service jobs, and in fact in any prominent place they wish to be. They say "consenting adults" have the right to choose their own life style. They claim they are not hurting anyone by their actions. In this they are badly mistaken. They are hurting young innocent

112

children if they are the teachers where your child goes to school. They are spoon-feeding this filth down young throats, an idea here, and a statement there, that is taking root in young minds. We have yet to see the consequence of such. Hopefully good people will wake up to what is being done and be vocal enough to assert *their* rights. Ladies, be on the alert against such blatant disregard for God's law. The Bible is our criterion. It is our standard. Do not let filthy minds, destitute of morality, determine what is right for you. Have enough conviction to say, "The Bible says . . ." It does not matter what man says, nor how much he sneers at the word of God. Just remember that when a man or woman wants to do wrong, he naturally would try to downgrade something that speaks out against what he wants to do.

Very recently I heard "Dear Abby" interviewed on the subject of homosexuality. She was asked the question, "If your young daughter came to you and said she was a homosexual, and wanted to continue this life style, what would you say or do?" Abby replied, "Twenty five years ago, I would have killed her. Now I would say to her, if this is the kind of life you want, I hope you will be very happy in it." This indelibly impresses upon my mind the truthfulness of the statement that our moral standards can change. Not only can, but have. Whereas if we used God's word for our standard then those moral standards always remain the same, regardless of what others are doing. It takes real courage in the face of a rebellious society to say, "The Bible says . . ." But we must. Just stay with God's word. Then morality takes on a significance that no man can destroy.

But now back to a study of other realms included in the word "chaste" about which we need to know:

*2. Indecent dress and actions:*

This can apply to both boys and girls, and should. However, in all fairness, I do think the women of our society are guiltier in this respect than boys. You may not agree; that is perfectly all right. But women can dress for the express purpose of arousing sexual urges in men. Men are more easily aroused than women, and for this reason the men do not dress to arouse passion in women. Girls, immodest clothing can cause this reaction in men. I know there are many instances of women being raped in which she was not at fault. But I also know that a large portion of the rape cases we hear about happen because some man has been sexually aroused by some woman in a bar, or at a beach. Her clothing was not adequate and the reaction was severe. It was probably much more severe than she ever dreamed about. I think even sweet, innocent girls can cause this same reaction and be totally unaware that they have done so.

Then there are those girls who deliberately set about to cause a reaction in men. They ask for it, and usually they get what they deserve. They can do this by dress, by subtle and sly movements of the body, by a look, or in any number of ways. Paul said to Timothy, "I desire therefore that women adorn themselves in modest apparel . . ." (1 Timothy 2:9). Discussed in a previous lesson was this word modest. Webster defines it as "decent. Observing the proprieties of dress and conduct." We cannot set the length in inches for the girls' skirts. What is proper and decent is going to have to be determined in every individual's eyes, and will not be observed unless that person has a proper concept of decency. But neither can we allow others to set the style or trend for us. Be of enough moral courage to set your own standards, right in your own eyes, based on what you think God would consider decent and appropriate for a christian, based also on a proper knowledge of human emotions and urges.

*3. Filthy language:*

We alone are responsible for the quality of conversation to which we listen. We alone are responsible for the quality of conversation we give out. What we feed into our minds is what comes out. Christ put it succinctly when He said, "But the things which proceed out of the mouth come forth out of the heart; and they defile the man. For out of the heart come forth evil thoughts, murders, adulteries, fornications, thefts, false witness, railings. These are the things which defile the man; but to eat with unwashen hands defileth not the man" (Matthew 15:18-20). So, young ladies, watch what you let seep into your ears, and so into your minds. It will eventually "out." Do not be guilty of being the one in the crowd who always has something filthy to say. I well remember a true story told by C. R. Nichol, gospel preacher. He said he was standing with a small group of men when one of them said, as he looked around, "Any ladies present?" He answered, "No, but there is a gentleman present," and walked off. Such avenues as movies, literature and television are prime avenues for garbage. There are a few good movies, much good literature, some good television if we will be selective. Too many times we are not. Any psychiatrist will tell you that we cannot listen to anything, read anything or see anything but that we are affected by it to some extent. Garbage will cause unchastity in your life and make you reprobate in the sight of God.

Some boys in a San Diego High School were asked to make a list of some of the things high school girls did that particularly annoyed them. They formed the following list and tacked it to the bulletin board. At first it made the girls mad, but the boys held their ground and noticed a definite improvement in a few days. Boys objected to:

1. Pettipants hanging out.

2. Skirts not long enough to cover underwear.

3. Carelessness when sitting with legs apart, or lying on floors.

4. Improper hose. Too short, can see hose tops, garters, bulging thighs.

5. Wearing masculine clothes — "Wear your own and let us wear ours."

6. Horrible make-up, frightening. Use a little, and learn how.

7. Vocabulary. Profane and obscene. Clean up your mouths or keep quiet.

8. Masculine actions — pushing, hitting, pounding on back, chasing, mussing our hair. Can't they just say "hello?"

9. Girls who are agressive, ask us for dates or to go steady, or do we love them.

10. Girls who come out at noon in skirts and try to play basketball or football with boys.

11. Girls who smoke, ditch classes, shoplift and hitch-hike are well-known to all of us, and respected by none.

115

In our next lesson we will continue with ways in which "unchastity" can manifest itself.

## Questions On
## LESSON NO. 10

1. What is the dictionary meaning of the word "chaste" and what is the Bible definition?

2. Is everyone obligated, as a christian, to acquire this quality of being chaste? In what respect does it confine itself peculiarly to women?

3. What are the two great rewards we have for being chaste?

4. Repeat the simple rule given in this lesson for our conduct as regards sexual relationships.

5. What are the five realms we have included in the definition of the word "chaste" which we are exploring in this lesson?

6. Name different ways in which sexual relationships can be wrong. Quote passages of scripture that deal with each.

7. What questions should a girl ask herself as to the "benefits" of indulging in these relationships?

8. Our "New Morality" teaches something far different from the Bible. What is it?

9. How can we violate the laws of chastity in dress and action?

10. Can we be unchaste in our language? How?

11. Name some of the things the boys in a San Diego High School objected to in some of the girls they watched daily.

# "Chaste"

In our last lesson we began a study on "chastity." We have already explored three avenues by which unchaste behavior can manifest itself: Unlawful sexual relationship, indecent dress, and filthy language. In this lesson we will conclude the chapter on "Chastity" with a study of immodesty other than indecent dress, and flamboyancy in our actions.

*4. Immodesty:*

Since we have discussed at some length the immodesty of dress, let us spend a little time on other ways in which immodesty can manifest itself, and how to avoid it. It is immodest to use vulgar language, filthy communications out of your mouth. Notice in the list of things boys hate to see in girls that two or three of these are related to immodesty in language. Besides just being plain obscene, girls can use words and expressions that are just simply not lady-like. Now that's an old-fashioned word, and one we seldom hear today, but it carries a lot of meaning even today. Of course we assume that no christian, either girl or boy, would want to engage in swearing or in telling filthy stories. But there are other expressions, rather innocent in themselves, that fit the vocabulary of a boy better than they do of a girl. Be dainty and feminine at all times. Do not give boys the impression that you are trying to take over their territory.

You can be immodest in aggressiveness. Contrary to all

we hear nowadays about women being on an equal with men, it is still true that most boys want to be the aggressor when it comes to asking for dates or making love. They like to be the ones who chase, not be the chased. Let the man take the lead in these things. It is his prerogative and it appeals to his manliness.

You can be immodest in the horrible habit of smoking. I go back far enough that I still shudder when I see a beautiful old gray-haired woman, nicely dressed, genteel-looking from every standpoint, do a very "un-genteel" thing. She reaches into her purse, pulls out a cigarette, leaves it dangling from those beautiful lips while she searches for a match, lights it and draws the smoke down deep into those delicate lungs. Somehow it seems so out of place. I think the women have outdone the men in this field within the past few years. Young women, do not begin this filthy habit. If you already have, determine to be the master of this weed and quit it now. From the standpoint of being injurious to the health, the total lack of femininity, a waste of money and time, and a very silly thing to do, you should not begin this habit. If you want to know what you should do about this, ask anyone who has smoked for years. Take that advice! I have no fear what it will be. Then remember that your example may cause someone to lightly esteem the Lord's church, or that you will bring reproach upon His cause. Your example is precious.

*5. Flamboyant in Actions:*

Checking our list again on the objections boys found by watching girls, we find that they listed "carelessness when sitting with legs apart, or lying on floors." They also talked about wearing masculine clothes, using masculine actions, pushing, hitting, pounding on the back, chasing, mussing the boys' hair. Most of these actions are commonly used by men but unbecoming in a woman. I have another peeve, seemingly innocent, but unbecoming somehow. It is that of loud, raucous laughter; laughter that is disagreeably harsh or strident, boisterous and disorderly. I have observed girls who actually believed they were attracting the attention of boys by such behavior, and they were! But not in the way they wished. A quiet and meek spirit is far better in the long run, and real boys will be attracted to feminine girls. Just give nature a chance.

How can a person learn to be "chaste?" How can she avoid all the pitfalls of unchastity? First ask yourself these probing questions:

"Do any of the things mentioned above, in which I might partake, destroy my identity as a christian?"

"Is it an offense to my conscience?" Paul said, "But he that doubteth is condemned if he eat, because he eateth not of faith; and whatsoever is not of faith is sin" (Romans 14:23). That means if you are a little doubtful that the thing you are doing is right, but do it anyway, you violate your conscience. Never do that! Always keep your conscience tender, else it will become seared if you violate it long enough, and it will not be pricked by any of your actions. If in doubt, leave it off!

"Will what I am doing cause others to sin?" Paul again said, "It is good not to eat flesh, nor to drink wine, nor to do anything whereby thy brother stumbleth" (Romans 14:21).

"Is it destructive to my body?" We learn, "Or know ye not that your body is a temple of the Holy Spirit which is in you, which ye have from God? and ye are not your own; for ye were bought with a price; glorify God therefore in your body" (1 Corinthians 6:19,20).

"Will it conflict or interfere with my duties as a christian?" Jesus told us, "But seek ye *first* the kingdom and his righteousness; and all these things shall be added unto you" (Matthew 6:33).

"Will it weaken my influence for good?" God has told us, "Prove all things; hold fast that which is good" (1 Thessalonians 5:21).

"Will it involve me in sinful association and bad company?" You can be sure of the result if you engage in it, since we learn, "Be not deceived: Evil companionships corrupt good morals" (1 Corinthians 15:33).

*READ THE BIBLE:*

How does one learn to be chaste? The Bible, if read faithfully, will give us the information we need in this field. Sir Wm. Jones wrote: "The Bible contains more true sublimity, more exquisite beauty, more pure morality, more important history, and finer strains of poetry and eloquence than can be collected from all other books in whatever age or language they may have been written." He expressed well the idea that if you want your language, your thoughts and your actions to be pure (chaste), apply yourself to knowing the Bible. "Finally, brethren, whatsoever things are true, whatsoever things are honorable, whatsoever things are just, whatsoever things are pure, whatsoever things are lovely, whatsoever things are of good report; if there be any virtue, and if there be any praise, *think on these things"* (Philippians 4:8).

Again, "And thou shalt write them upon the doorposts of thy house, and upon thy gates" (Deuteronomy 6:9).

And finally, "Let not kindness and truth forsake thee. Bind them about thy neck; write them upon the tablet of thy heart" (Proverbs 3:3).

### SOME THINGS OF WHICH TO BEWARE:

By being knowledgeable of the likely pitfalls we can better avoid them. A person walking in a dark house can better avoid stumbling over some piece of furniture if she knows where each piece is. A person driving down a rough road may hit every hole the first trip across, but after acquainting himself with the whereabouts of the worst ones his succeeding trips can be smoother. So it is with pitfalls in life. There are two ways of learning about pitfalls; one by experiencing them, and the second by learning what they are from others who have had the bad experiences and have given us the benefit of their knowledge. A wise person can profit from reading and learning of others mistakes.

Let's list some of the pitfalls:

*1. Petting:* Petting incites passion. It is not smart, but dumb. It is not wise, but foolish. It is not modern, but old as the hills, and it leads to sinful actions. Modesty, virtue and chastity are not old-fashioned and out-of-date. Men still want a good clean wife. God wrote a book for men of all ages, and He knows what is best for us; he wants us to be happy. When boys tell you that you will no longer be popular unless you agree to go along with his desires, have the fortitude and moral

121

conviction to tell him being popular is not important to you. If a boy ignores restraints he will not make a good husband anyway. The sooner you lose him, the better off you will be.

How do we solve the problem of avoiding these sins? Read the list: "Fornication, uncleanness, lasciviousness, idolatry, sorcery, enmities, strife, jealousies, wraths, factions, divisions, parties, envyings, drunkenness, revellings, and such like" (Galatians 5:19-21). Horrible sins these are, which must be avoided. Just say "no" and mean it; stay with it. It is a very simple, but a very effective solution to any pitfall we may encounter. I would stress the fact that it is not a very wise thing for a young girl to start going steady until she has reached the maturity that has no difficulty in making the right decisions. Going steady naturally breeds familiarity, and your chances of being alone together are increased. Saying "no" might be very difficult under some circumstances. Mothers, you can help in situations like this by being very sure your immature girl is not left alone with boys for long periods of time, with no adult there for proper supervision.

*2. Dancing:* Dancing is defined as a rhythmical movement of any or all parts of the body. It falls into the category of "works of the flesh" mentioned in Galatians 5. We have a society in which dancing becomes part of the school program at a very early age in your life, or in the life of your child. Christians have been up against a stone wall for many years on this question, especially in relation to their school program. My full sympathy is with them. It is a struggle. But we find we must fight sin in every area, not just in dancing. So this is just another area in which christians must take their stand. As yet your child is not compelled to join in, if he is forbidden by the parents. If it gets to that, then we must still obey God rather than man. We used to be asked questions about dancing by young people more than we are now. I really do not know why they have quit asking. Maybe they have decided to go ahead and dance. I hope this is not the case. Regardless of the type of dance, and the bodily contact, the very motions of the body are sensuous and suggestive. It is designed to excite and arouse passions. Many girls have been led off the dance floor into parked cars for a riotous exercise

122

of love-making, simply because the boy had been over-excited and aroused on the dance floor. Honestly now, if dances were conducted for boys only, or girls only, would they take place?

Dancing has been referred to as "the walking embrace." This is reveling in a true sense of the word. Just try to write out a definition of "reveling" some time and omit any reference to the dance. Lastly, it appeals solely to the flesh, and destroys spirituality. I heard a story many years ago, but even in our society today I think it would be apropos:

A young lady, a member of the church, had upheld her idea of dancing, denying that it was a worldly, sinful exercise. She wanted to attend a dance, but her parents were opposed. Finally they asked her to talk to the preacher about it. At the close of their talk, seeing that he had made no headway in changing her mind, the preacher said, "All right, I'll give my sanction to your attending this dance tonight if you will just do one thing for me." The girl, thinking she had won the argument, eagerly answered, "Sure, what is it?" The preacher replied, "While you are dancing with your escort, just ask him if he is a christian." The girl agreed. While they were dancing she found that it was much more difficult to bring up that subject than she had anticipated. But she had agreed, so getting up her nerve she asked, "Are you a christian?" He backed off an arm's length, looked at her aghast, and answered, "NO, are you?" She said, "Yes, I am." He answered, "Well, what are you doing here?" This gives you an idea of what the world expects from a christian. No matter what our society teaches in the way of accepting this activity, no christian should want to engage in it, and certainly should avoid dancing as one of the pitfalls toward unchastity.

Some additional thoughts on the subject of dancing can be suggested in the form of these questions. Try to be objective and answer them fairly:

1. Does it incite me to unlawful thoughts and desires?

2. Does it incite my partner?

3. Does it lead to baser things definitely forbidden by God?

4. Does it increase the respect good people have for me?

5. Does it increase my love for God?

6. Does it make me delight in reading the Bible?

7. Does it lead me to pray more?

8. Does it increase my zeal for the spread of the Lord's church?

9. Does it make me a better christian?

10. Would my friends on the dance floor be surprised to know I am a christian?

Most of the above questions could be asked about the other questionable activities in which some people find themselves embroiled. Better watch out! The trap is set and you might ensnare yourself in one of these hurtful, dubious activities.

Make up your mind that as a christian you cannot afford to engage in questionable practices. Let there be no doubt in your mind or anyone else's that all your actions evolve from a desire to live a pure, clean, chaste life. Give the world, especially your associates, the picture of a chaste, godly woman. Who knows, this might influence someone to want to be like you, a christian. What an influence a godly life can wield. One can have many close friends and be a christian. You do not have to lead the life of a hermit. You may have to select other friends, but believe me, some good people, likeable and fun to be with, are still around trying to serve God. I heard a man say, who had been a member of the church only a short time, "I didn't know what having fun was until I became a christian. I used to think when I was doing all those sinful things that I was having fun. But now I know I wasn't."

"A clean mind, a clear conscience and a sincere determination to live a righteous life is a constant source of happiness. The pleasures of sin are only for a season and then comes the harvest of anxiety, remorse, regret and shame. A clean life produces courage and confidence and brings great blessings, both here and hereafter. If you would be truly happy, always live a righteous life." [Author Unknown]

Lastly, follow these four rules for a happy, chaste life:

1. Give heed to God's word (Deuteronomy 6:9; Proverbs 3:3).

2. Keep your thoughts clean (Philippians 4:8).

124

3. Strive for purity of speech, foregoing profanity and obscenity (Ephesians 4:29)

4. Keep your body undefiled (1 Corinthians 6:19).

## Questions On
## LESSON NO. 11

1. In what other areas than dress and language can a girl be unchaste, or immodest?

2. What about being flamboyant in our actions? What does this include?

3. Discuss the value of being aware of pitfalls.

4. What are some of the questions we might ask ourselves before engaging in any activity?

5. Why are we admonished so much to read and study the Bible?

6. Discuss some of the pitfalls associated with petting.

7. How does modern living contribute to the ease young couples have in the activity of petting?

8. In your opinion is dancing wrong? If so, why? If not, why?

9. How is the best way to present a picture of a chaste woman to the world?

10. Would being the kind of person God wants you to be make you without friends? Would it make you unhappy?

11. Discuss the four rules for a happy, chaste life.

# Chapter Five      Lesson 12

# "Workers at Home"

### Homemaking

In our present modern world the art of homemaking is almost an old-fashioned phrase. Can a woman in this period of time find fulfillment and happiness in this role? Yes, she most definitely can. She was made by God to fulfill this role. She has every qualification for it. In the passage of scripture from which these lessons have been formed, Titus 2:3-5, she is commanded by God to do it. Young women are "admonished to rule the household" (1 Timothy 5:14). Since we know that God desires our happiness, and since we know God has not asked us to do anything that would make us unhappy, it follows that being good homemakers, if properly done, will bring about our greatest happiness in this world, even in our present world.

Housework can be a boring and fretting occupation. You dust the furniture and lo! and behold! you look at the table-tops the next day or so and they need dusting again. There is not a great deal of pure, physical pleasure to be derived from taking a dust cloth, or a vacuum, and removing dirt from table-tops. Then in what respect do we find happiness in these chores? In knowing that we are accomplishing our part in the bargain we made when we vowed to be "keepers at home." Think about your husband on his job. Do you not think he finds and does boring jobs over and over? Then in what sense does he find happiness in his work?

127

In knowing that he is providing for his family, and the pure sense of accomplishment in a job well done.

I was impressed when we recently flew, and especially in the light of preparing this lesson, by watching the airline stewardesses as they went about their jobs. Most girls have the impression that being an airline stewardess is a thrilling occupation. But most of what they did was dull and routine. From the moment we enplaned they were going through the procedure of showing passengers how to use their safety equipment or serving food and drink. The balance of the trip was filled with these dull, routine duties. I couldn't really say that what they were doing was any more thrilling than keeping my home from day to day.

So very important to your role of homemaking is your attitude toward it. There are so many moments of real enjoyment, especially the over-all picture of accomplishment. We should be *proud* of our roles and seek to find our happiness in this field. Think of the real blessings you will enjoy. First, in knowing you have done God's will, and secondly in seeing the gleam of sincere love in your husband's eyes as he enjoys a meal carefully and lovingly prepared by you. Think of the blessing of caring for your children, watching them grow and develop. Think of the pure pleasure derived from a shining and lovely home when you have finished the work of cleaning. This will be a real home where a husband finds release from the everyday world, a rest and relaxation and haven that soothes his tired nerves and fits him for another day in the work-a-day world.

In becoming a real homemaker, remember these things:

*Don't put off doing what needs to be done.* If you do, then you will be forced to do it too rapidly and that will cause you to be edgy and ill-tempered about it. It will cause you to lose the joy of doing.

*Go the second mile! Do your jobs well!* You can learn this by doing. It will make an easier job for you. Not only will your husband appreciate it and praise you, but you will enjoy it yourself.

Good home-making serves as a good stimulus in the development of your character. Doing unliked tasks properly

128

and without grudging will make a better person of you. If you have a dirty job to do, something you are really dreading, make up your mind to get that job done as soon as possible and as well as possible. Then you do not have to dread that any more and you have become more resolute in your duty. See how much better you feel already? After all, we are all striving for the proper development of character, and this will help.

CONCENTRATION on any job helps alleviate tedium and difficulty. When you arise in the morning and you know certain household chores need to be done that day, take the time to sit down and organize your work. What are your priorities? What needs doing the most or the first? Then begin with that and try not to get side-tracked. It is so easy to let something interfere, and especially if we have a job we do not particularly relish. But sticking to it will develop the quality of stedfastness and get the job over with sooner. Coffee with the neighbors every morning after the family is off to work and school can get to be a time-consuming habit, and one hard to break. I never felt that I had the time for this. There is nothing wrong, per se, with having another cup of coffee with the neighbors. Especially is this true if you think there might be an opportunity to teach. But for idle chit-chat, pure social get-togethers, I consider it a waste of time. First of all get that job done! And then if you have time, do other things.

Exceptions to the rule of organization is "priorities." If there is a sick child, a neighbor or member of the church that needs visiting, or needs food taken in, this would take priority over any household chore. Even a day off now and then for pure relaxation, shopping, something you do only now and then would be allowable. These rare occasions should not change the course of your regular routine.

CLUTTER: Avoid it like the plague! I have seen houses so filled with "things," there was not one square inch on a table-top to set anything down. I remember a statement made by a preacher who held meetings continuously, and stayed in all kinds of homes. He said some places had so many bouquets of paper and plastic flowers he couldn't find room to set his shaving equipment down, much less to write an article or a letter. In one house we counted as many as thirty-six bouquets of plastic flowers in one room. Yes, a home needs little touches of beauty that you can supply, but learn that simplicity in decoration is beautiful, and in good taste.

*LEARN TO WORK:* It will not hurt you; it will do you good. It is not above the dignity of a virtuous woman to work hard with her hands. Remember the example of the "worthy woman" in Proverbs?

## Some of Our Household Chores

*COOKING* is one of the duties imposed on a homemaker. Personally, I love to cook. I like it so well that I have often made cakes we do not need, taking them to the freezer to use later for company. I like to bake my own bread. I do not claim any credit for the achievement I may have attained in the field of cooking, because I do it for the pure pleasure of doing it. Others may have other fields of homemaking in which they delight. But one thing I know about cooking is that meals prepared from scratch are the best. Prepare well-balanced meals, on time, well prepared. Men like hearty dishes like beef stew, roast beef and potatoes, fried chicken and gravy, biscuits, crisp green salads, apple pie and ice cream. They dislike cold cuts and T.V. dinners. They like things that smell good cooking. You know what they are. Give them this homey pleasure. Your children will like it, too. I can still remember the cold winter days when I walked a mile from my elementary school to my home. As I entered the house I could smell gingerbread cooking. Mother had an old wood-burning range, and a big square pan that she always used for gingerbread. She didn't cook it every day, but the days she did were highlights of the month. We took it out of the oven piping hot, lavished a bit of butter on it. Mmm! the mouthwatering goodness! No doubt all of you have similar memories. You can give memories to your children, too.

*SEWING:* I am glad to see the trend back toward sewing. My hat is off to young girls who will do this. Only recently someone told me of a young girl about twelve years of age who could make a dress for herself amost as well as her

130

mother could, and her mother is an accomplished seamstress. You can save your husband a lot of money by doing your own sewing, and be nicely dressed at the same time. In learning this art you will need also to learn which styles become *you,* and which colors look best on you. All this contributes to the overall picture of a well-groomed, feminine woman.

*HANDLING MONEY:* There are many ways to make a dollar stretch. Buy good materials, nothing cheap or shoddy, take care of things making them last a long time.

Buy good food, in the largest practical size. Goods that will keep can be purchased in large economy sizes, as they are usually more inexpensive. If they are perishable and will not be eaten soon, buying in large sizes is a waste of money. Prepared foods are always higher so learn to cook from scratch. People have to be paid a high salary to prepare your foods ahead of time for you. Do it yourself at home. Cheaper cuts of meat are sometimes a bargain, sometimes not. Learn to shop wisely. A roast with lots of bone and fat is sometimes more of a waste than a meaty roast, but with a higher price. Some lower cuts of meat are good bargains, but may have to cook longer to be tender. But it can be done, and in some instances should.

If you have space and time, raise a garden. Don't go overboard, but do raise a few of the things you like best. Even a tomato plant or two in the flower bed will give you lots of help on that budget.

Avoid buying every gadget that comes on the market. Television is such a good source of advertising, and the housewife is the prime target. A clever salesman can demonstrate a knife, a slicer, a grater, or any kind of gadget so well that the housewife thinks she just must have that. It looks easy on television. The demonstration is designed to make you want to buy. In a few years you can have drawers full of gadgets that you never use. If you don't think this is true, come to my house and open my kitchen cabinet drawers. *I didn't need them!* I learned the hard way. Maybe you can profit from my mistakes.

### Other Areas in Which a Wife Can Provide
*The Physical Needs of the Husband:*

131

The wife should have the proper attitude toward fulfilling this need. It should be met willingly and lovingly. It is the wife's responsibility to see that this phase of the marriage relationship is fulfilled. A wife should never use "sex" as a weapon, withholding it to get something she wants. This is childish and selfish. So many pages of the New Testament are filled with admonitions prohibiting adultery and fornication. God knew that this urge is one of the greatest human urges in man. He should know, because He made us, and He knows our frame. In a former lesson we found that because of the indulgence of this urge in illicit ways, great nations have been led to ruin. But the urge is there and it is God-given. God has never saddled man with any natural urge that cannot be satisfied lawfully. The lawful means for this urge is within the scope of the marriage bond. Outside of marriage God gives no sanction to the satisfying of this urge. The young woman who is contemplating marriage, or any woman for that matter, should learn this lesson well. Love is not *just* sex, but without it love is never fully satisfied nor complete. You want your husband to remain faithful to you, not to have illicit relationships with other women. But if you deny him, you may cause him to be tempted to seek his satisfaction elsewhere. Resolve now to make your marriage a happy one in this respect. If you willingly and lovingly give him this love your marriage will be rewarded a thousand times over. If I had to stress any one facet of marriage this would certainly be placed at the top. As I stated before, it is certainly not the whole of marriage, but it does fill a great need of the man, and only the wife can do this for him legitimately. He can *hire* a housekeeper, he can *hire* a companion, he can take a girl out to dinner, and he can have a lively, intelligent conversation, but only a wife can satisfy this desire as God would have it satisfied. Paul tells us, "But because of fornications, let each man have his own wife, and let each woman have her own husband. Let the husband render unto the wife her due; and likewise also the wife unto her husband" (1 Corinthians 7:2,3). "Defraud ye not one the other, except it be by consent for a season, that ye may give yourselves unto prayer, and may be together again, *that Satan tempt you not because*

132

*of your incontinency"* (1 Corinthians 7:5).

## Your Mental Stability

For the mental needs of your husband, the wife needs to maintain her mental alertness by the continuous feeding of her mind on a variety of subjects. By this I do not mean that a wife must be well-informed on every subject. But be alert to what is going on in the world. Read articles on world affairs. Do not be so consumed with household duties that you lose sight of affairs of government, travel, local politics, the school situation, the business world, and above all, things that pertain to your husband's work. There are instances in which he would like to discuss with you some of the things concerning his job: not that he needs you to take over for him, but that you can create an atmosphere of intelligent "listening." You can supply an idea here or there, or sympathize with him if he has problems. A good "listening post" does much to relieve the tensions he may have.

## Your Spiritual Encouragement and Growth

Aquila and Priscilla, husband and wife, taught God's word side by side (Acts 18:24-26). Zacharias and Elizabeth, husband and wife, were both righteous before God, walking in all the commandments and ordinances of the Lord blameless (Luke 1:5,6). Two together, working side by side for their spiritual development, will help each other to grow. Helping to accomplish this goal can be made easier by the wife if she will create the following activities:

1. Arrange for a quiet place conducive to his study of God's word.

2. Plan regular periods for Bible study together.

3. Help and encourage him to qualify for the eldership, or as a deacon, or to preach the gospel and aid in the teaching program (1 Timothy 3:11).

4. Encourage him to actively participate in public worship.

5. Be submissive and obedient. That will encourage his spiritual growth.

6. You can be a great influence in "doing good to all men" (Galatians 6:10).

7. If *you* are growing spiritually it will stimulate him to grow spiritually.

## Questions On
## LESSON NO. 12

1. Can a woman find fulfillment in the role of home-maker?  How?

2. Did God so instruct women?  Where?

3. Name some ways that will stimulate our growth and development in homemaking.

4. Give us your idea of the kind of home you would like to have.  Are you willing to work to make it this kind?

5. Of all the jobs of homemaking which do you like best? Worst?  Why?

6. Name other areas about which we need to be learning.

7. Why is it necessary to learn to do these?

8. Are you afraid of the sex relationship?  Can you learn from a study about it?

9. In what way does God let man legitimately satisfy this urge?

10. What responsibility does this place on the wife?

11. How can we learn to help out financially?

12. Are there other areas in which a wife can help provide for her husband?  What are they?

13. In your opinion, why is it important to develop together spiritually?

# Chapter Six    Lesson 13

# "To Be Kind"

*KINDNESS:* The very word itself denotes qualities of tenderness and affection; of consideration for our fellows; gentleness and compassion. What a superb characteristic of the christian woman! How good it would be if the remembrance of each of us could be the quality of kindness. Webster defines kindness as "having feelings befitting our common nature; benevolent; well-disposed; gracious. Proceeding from, or characterized by goodness or benevolence. Gentle, tractable." All these words conjure up in our minds the sort of person God wants us to be. Paul, by the direction of the Holy Spirit, wrote to a young preacher, Titus. Paul gave Titus a message to convey to older women on the island of Crete. These older women were in turn to teach it to the young women. Kindness was part of the message that God wanted young women to develop.

Kindness can be cultivated. It is a feminine trait, though men possess it, too. But with women we see it as part of the feminine role. A curt, brusk, cruel woman is entirely out of character. Once in a while we see women assuming a role like this but it is obviously out of line; so much so that usually it provokes comment. David acknowledged that God displayed the quality of kindness toward him when he said, "Blessed be Jehovah; for He hath showed me his marvelous loving-kindness in a strong city" (Psalms 31:21).

Acts of kindness can manifest themselves in various ways. Do you really care about people? Are you concerned when they are in need? In the book of Acts we have a marvelous example of a good woman who cared. Dorcas, or Tabitha, was skillful as a seamstress. She made and gave away many garments, especially to widows. The account says of her, "This woman was full of good works and almsdeeds which she did" (Acts 9:36).

Dorcas died, and since Peter was nearby at Lydda, the disciples sent for him. When he came, the widows gathered around him weeping and showing the coats and garments Dorcas had made for them while she was with them.

This was their response to the kindness this good woman had shown them. It is nice to read that Peter, by the power given him by the Holy Spirit, raised this good woman from the dead and presented her back to them alive. What joy they must have felt! What love her kindness had prompted in their hearts!

Kindness not only can be developed, but it can be taught. Parents can teach their children to be kind; kind to their pets, kind to other children, to parents, to grandparents, and to other adults. We see various degrees of this quality displayed by children. Not always are we fully able to tell if children are just plain rude, or if they are just plain bashful. We can overlook a lot of rudeness in a child if there is some indication that the parent is making an effort to teach them kindness. Be patient and wait for this quality to develop. It won't come overnight. Like other good qualities it will be worth waiting for and working toward. Then there will come the day when that child will mature to the point where all the hard teaching pays off, and you can sit back and admire your product, a fine young girl or boy who at last shows qualities of kindness and consideration. You, too, no matter what your age, can develop and grow in this characteristic. Begin now to analyze your actions, and really ask yourself the question: Am I kind to people? Do I really care if they have problems? Have I ever taken the time to *ask* if they are troubled? When I do ask, and they start to confide in me some problem that is troubling them, do I listen? Do I hear it, and do something about it? This is a matter of training. The more you work at it, the easier it will become. Your ear will soon learn the knack of being attuned to others' misfortunes.

Take time to do that one little thing that will mean so much to someone. Did you write that letter to a friend of long standing? Did you send that card to someone who was sick? Did you visit that shut-in who so desperately needed a visit? Did you find some older person to take out to lunch, who would so love to go?

Kindness is enjoined by God in his Holy Word. Read the book of Ruth. Ruth, because of her kindness toward her mother-in-law, Naomi, was likewise treated with kindness by Boaz. She later was married to Boaz, through which lineage Jesus Christ was born. In our study of the "worthy woman," we find that "the law of kindness was on her tongue" (Proverbs 31:26). Paul admonishes christians to be ministers of God "in kindness . . ." (2 Corinthians 6:6). And again he tells us, "And be ye kind one to another, tenderhearted, forgiving each other, even as God also in Christ forgave you" (Ephesians 4:32). Again, "Put on therefore, as God's elect, holy and beloved, a heart of compassion, kindness . . ." (Colossians 3:12). And lastly, "Love suffereth long and is kind . . ." (1 Corinthians 13:4).

In summary, therefore, we stress the fact that this quality of kindness, enjoined by the Lord, can be acquired and maintained if we work at it and develop ourselves. If we want to be truly feminine women, we must develop traits that will make us so.

"To him that is ready to faint kindness should be showed" (Job 6:14). Now watch how the two qualities·of "kindness" and "truth" are joined together in this next scripture, "Let not kindness and truth forsake thee: Bind them about thy neck; write them upon the tablet of thy heart: *so* shalt thou find favor and good understanding in the sight of God and man" (Proverbs 3:3). What a forceful way of saying that a christian should at all times maintain kindness. Let us be found, not only in the paths of truth, but also in the paths of kindness. God enjoins both upon us in this scripture.

1. Give several synonyms for the word kindness.

2. Is kindness just a feminine trait? Should it be cultivated by women? Why?

3. Name some ways in which acts of kindness can manifest themselves.

4. Must this trait of kindness be developed, or is it spontaneous?

5. In what way can we develop the trait?

6. Did God enjoin kindness on his children? Quote passages.

7. What forceful way did Solomon have in expressing the quality of kindness?

# Chapter Seven    Lesson 14

# "Being in Subjection to Their Own Husbands"

Being in subjection means something. Words are not put in the Bible to fill up space. Just as any other command in the Bible, this one is important. The young woman will want to know what it means that she may fully accept and obey it. This lesson in some phases overlaps the first lessons we studied on our relationships to our husbands, but in this lesson we want to re-emphasize our place in God's scheme or order, and better know what it means to "be in subjection."

Remember again: "God knows our frame." He made us, and he knows what is best for us. If he stipulated that the woman should be in subjection to the man he did it for our benefit. Of course we *want* the benefits of God's love, so this command needs to be studied.

In the light of modern-day thinking and teaching, the present-day Women's Liberation Movement, and the growing tendency among women to be independent of men, there is an even greater need for a thorough study and teaching on this subject. Christians will not rebel at this clear teaching of the scripture.

To begin with, we have Adam and Eve in the garden of Eden. Eve was enticed by the devil and ate of the fruit of the tree of knowledge of good and evil. Then she gave to her husband, Adam, and he ate of it. Thus sin came into the world. When God encountered them in the garden and knew

139

they had violated his direct command, He pronounced the death sentence upon them. They died spiritually (separated from God) that very day, and they began to die physically from that day forward, being separated from the tree of life. To Adam God said, "Because thou hast hearkened unto the voice of thy wife, and hast eaten of the tree, of which I commanded thee, saying, Thou shalt not eat of it: cursed is the ground for thy sake; in toil shalt thou eat of it all the days of thy life; thorns also and thistles shall it bring forth to thee; and thou shalt eat the herb of the field; in the sweat of thy face shalt thou eat bread, till thou return unto the ground; for out of it wast thou taken; for dust thou art, and unto dust shalt thou return" (Genesis 3:17-19). This would be Adam's punishment.

Then upon Eve God pronounced this punishment: "I will greatly multiply thy pain and thy conception; in pain thou shalt bring forth children; and *thy desire shall be to thy husband, and he shall rule over thee"* (Genesis 3:16).

Just as surely as man cannot bring forth food from the earth without toil, sweat, weeds, thistles and thorns, just that surely woman cannot bring forth young without pain, and just that surely she is to be in subjection to her husband. This is a law of God that cannot be refuted. We do not bear the sin of Adam and Eve, but we *must* bear the consequence of their sin. We are living with the consequence.

To show that this law is incorporated into the law of Christ we turn to a wealth of passages that so state:

"Wives, be in subjection unto your own husbands, as unto the Lord" (Ephesians 5:22-23). Read the whole passage and see how many times, and in other ways, this idea is expressed.

"Wives, be in subjection to your husbands, as is fitting in the Lord" (Colossians 3:18).

"In like manner, ye wives, be in subjection to your own husbands . . ." (1 Peter 3:1). Continue the reading of the passage in 1 Peter 3 to underscore the idea of subjection.

We are using a text throughout this study that emphasizes the subjection of women to men, and states in the last phrase, "that the word of God be not blasphemed" (Titus 2:5). When we disobey any of the commands in God's word, and now expressly in this study when we disobey God's command to be in subjection, we are guilty of having blasphemed the word of God. Surely we do not want to do that. So we must learn subjection.

Paul gives us the proper order as God would have it: "But I would have you know, that the head of every man is Christ; and the head of the woman is the man; and the head of Christ is God" (1 Corinthians 11:3). It adds up to: GOD, CHRIST, MAN, WOMAN, in that order. He gives the reason: "For Adam was first formed, then Eve" (1 Timothy 2:13).

When Paul is discussing this subject, his main thrust is the picture of the church as the bride of Christ being in subjection to Christ, the bridegroom (Ephesians 5). We as christians recognize the fact that Christ is the head of the church and rules over his kingdom. He makes the laws concerning his kingdom, we are subjects in his kingdom, and he has *all authority* over his kingdom. Giving the great commission Jesus said, "*All authority* hath been given unto me in heaven and on earth. Go ye therefore, and make disciples of all the nations, baptizing them into the name [authority] of the Father, and of the Son and of the Holy Spirit" (Matthew 28: 18-20).

"And in none other is there salvation [in any other name than Christ]: for neither is there any other name [authority] under heaven, that is given among men, wherein we must be saved" (Acts 4:12).

"These shall war against the Lamb, and the Lamb shall overcome them, for he is Lord of lords, and King of kings ..." (Revelation 17:14). He is the greatest of all rulers and has all authority.

God's own testimony concerning Christ's position is, "Which he wrought in Christ when he raised him from the dead, and made him to sit at his right hand in the heavenly places, far above all rule, and authority, and power, and dominion, and every name that is named, not only in this world, but also in that which is to come: and he put all things *in subjection* under his feet, and gave him to be *head* over all things to the church, which is his body, the fulness of him that filleth all in all" (Ephesians 1:20-23). So just as Christ, the bridegroom, has the right to this authority over the church, his bride, so in like manner God gave the bridegroom, man, authority over his bride, woman.

## Subjection

What is meant by "subjection?" It simply means that there is someone *over* you in authority. We are in subjection to the laws of our land, to civil authority. Paul said, "Let every soul be in subjection to the higher powers [civil authority] . . ." (Romans 13:1). This verse uses the exact phrase, "in subjection." This does not mean that we are not "free" people. We live in a "land of the free." In our country, we are not in slavery to any man. But "freedom" is impossible without "law." If this were not so, we would live in a state of anarchy. Anarchy simply means "absence of government . . . a state of lawlessness." We are not "free" to take money not belonging to us, nor to disobey any other law of the land. We think for ourselves, we have certain inalienable rights, we discuss matters that concern us, and we have freedom of choice in voting for candidates we think would serve us best. We are not under a dictator and are not slaves. The church, under Christ, is "free." Paul said, "For he that was called in the Lord, being a bondservant, is the Lord's freedman: likewise he that was called being free, is Christ's bondservant" (1 Corinthians 7:22). Galatians 4 gives us a good lesson on what it means to be the Lord's freedman. The old law was likened to the state of slavery, and the law of Christ to being free. But even though these passages teach that we are free , everyone recognizes that God has law. James talks about the "law of liberty" (James 1:25). Christ has laid down certain laws that must be followed if we are pleasing to God and acceptable in his sight.

So this is what we mean by the human relationship of marriage. The husband is the head of the family. The wife is in subjection, second to him. Their relationship is, or should be, based on love. A likeness of the marriage relationship is expressed in the creation when God took from the side of Adam a rib, and with it formed a woman. It is symbolic that God did not take the bone from Adam's head, that he should be a dictator, and she the slave. But he took it from his side, that she would become a loving companion; walking with him down the pathway of life. When properly followed this is a beautiful relationship. But it gets out of hand when the woman attempts to usurp the man's rightful authority and rule over him. On the other hand, a man is out of line when he begins to over-exert his authority, much in the master-slave concept.

As in a big business concern where one man is the president and has absolute authority in making and enforcing the rules of that company, so it is in the home. If the business-man is wise, he will delegate to others the authority to carry out various phases of the work. They are given fields in which to operate, making the necessary decisions. But the final decision and the overall plan for the success of that business is his.

In the church God has placed Christ in the position of King. The King makes the rules and has given us the blue-print for the work and worship of each local congregation. But his authority has given us elders over each church. They cannot, dare not, change Christ's blueprint, nor make the laws of their own. They cannot, dare not, change Christ's laws governing his church. But they do have the right, the authority, as far as the local work of that church is concerned, to carry out Christ's law in the best judgment they can execute.

So, in the family relationship, the husband should be the head of the family. The overall planning and his judgment of what he wants his family to be and do should be carried out. In this scheme is his plan for the execution of the home duties. This is the realm in which the wife operates, over which she reigns as queen. He wants and expects her to operate in this capacity: the preparation of meals, the planning and purchasing of clothing for the family, the operation of the home in every detail is hers. He normally would not choose to be concerned or bothered with the details of these things. But still it should be his plan that is being wisely executed by a woman of intelligence. In the business world, the owner or president of that company would expect the men selected to make certain decisions to be able to perform. So in the home, the husband expects the wife to be able to perform her duties, and an intelligent and capable wife will do that very thing to the best of her ability.

A man and his wife should have an understanding of how much money can be spent on household expenses, and should be able to carry out this arrangement in a simple, business-like way. Each couple may have a different method of budgeting their money, and the arrangement is up to them, but a clear understanding between husband and wife is imperative. Then when the arrangement is complete the wife has leeway to spend that money as wisely and in the direction that she deems best. This is authority used by the wife in agreement with the husband to better facilitate the running of the household. I have known some men who did all the shopping for the family; the clothing, both for the wife and the children, the household furnishing, and even the groceries. Not knowing the reason for such I would not pronounce judgment. It may be that the wife failed at her task. But by and large, most men would prefer not to be bothered with the details of household management. They are glad to have a wise and cautious wife to manage these things for them. It does place a burden on the wife, and does behoove her to act in the wisest way possible to be worthy of the trust of her husband.

There will be one more lesson in this series, but with this lesson we conclude the teaching given in our verses of scripture, which tells us, "That aged women likewise be reverent in demeanor, not slanderers nor enslaved to much wine, teachers of that which is good; that they may train the young women to love their husbands, to love their children, to be sober-minded, chaste, workers at home, kind, being in subjection to their own husbands, that the word of God be not blasphemed" (Titus 2:3-5).

We trust the lessons have been profitable to you, and that you can now say that you are better equipped to take your place in the home and fulfill your God-given role in the manner acceptable to God and to your husband. We pray that we have accomplished this. There will be yet one more lesson on just practical suggestions, based solely on our observations and experiences. Opinions have little worth in the study

144

of God's word, so we ask that you bear with us through the next lesson. It may be that you can profit by the observations.

May God richly bless each of you as you launch forth into this world. Our prayer for you is that you may find a richness, fulness, and a most rewarding life, both here and hereafter.

## Questions On
## LESSON NO. 14

1. Is "being in subjection" a condition that would be degrading to an individual? Name some instances in which man is in subjection.

2. What is the arrangement God made with Adam and Eve in the garden?

3. Does this same law hold true in the New Testament? Quote passages.

4. What does "in subjection" mean?

5. Give us your comments on how big businesses are run.

6. What about being "in subjection" to civil authority?

7. How does being "in subjection" apply in the arrangement with Christ and His church?

8. In the family relationship how is this pattern extended?

9. Does such a relationship become degrading to a woman?

10. Give some practical suggestions on budgeting in the home, and how best to carry out God's arrangement for the home.

# Lesson 15

# Practical Suggestions

In studying the foregoing lessons we trust that we have not inserted our opinions. We have tried to base our conclusions on the scripture. We have used the text, Titus 2:3-5, for the chapter headings in our study. Seven chapters, with headings found in these two verses of scripture: (1) Love Their Husbands, (2) Love Their Children, (3) Be Sober-Minded, (4) Chaste, (5) Workers At Home, (6) Kind, (7) In Subjection to Their Own Husbands, that the word of God be not blasphemed.

But now in the realm of "practical suggestions" we want to leave you with these thoughts, found not in our scripture, but based on our observations, experiences, and over-all teaching of the word of God. In achieving the role of the woman God would have you be there are some suggestions that will make your job easier and bring you to a better understanding of what is expected of you.

1. Above all things begin now a regular, consistent, thorough study of the word of God. There is nothing in this world that will give you a more complete education than this. God has given to his creation a plan of perfection. By perfection we do not mean that we ever reach the state that we are above sin. Perfection is used in the sense of "maturing" or "growing up in Him." God desires his children to have this fullness, this maturity, this completeness. You can accomplish

147

this by having a set time each day for Bible *study*. When I emphasize study, I have a reason. Just a mere reading of words will accomplish a little. But a meditation upon, and a thorough study of, will accomplish more.

2. *Be a woman. Dress* like one, act like one, think like one. This covers a lot of territory. The women's liberation movement would have us believe the ideal arrangement is toward a "unisex." There is no such thing. God made them "male and female." Be satisfied with God's arrangement, and profit by it. Let the men be men, but you be a woman. Soft clothing, feminine touches like ruffles, lace, scarves, ribbons, flowers and jewelry just naturally make you think of women. The trend nowadays is toward copying men's styles. If the men have pants, vest, coat, hat then it isn't long until women have pants, vest, coat and hat, all made almost identical to the men's style.

*Talk* like a woman. A soft voice, not loud and strident, becomes a woman. Masculine gestures, such as back-slapping, should be avoided.

Maintain *good health*. Acquire good habits of eating, sleeping, exercise. You will feel better and present to the world a fresh, wholesome look. If you feel good physically, it will cause you to have a better mental outlook also.

Don't use *excessive make-up*. Be judicious and subtle. Too much powder, eye-shadow, rouge, mascara or lipstick is not natural and looks gawdy.

Be *childlike*. Don't become blase or calloused. Learn to appreciate simple things. Have that child-like quality of trusting, being open and frank with people. Jesus said, "Except ye turn, and become as little children . . ." He was not saying that we should remain as a child mentally or spiritually, but that there are certain traits we would do well to retain. A child is teachable, he is not malicious or spiteful. If he quarrels with a playmate it is soon over and forgotten. Paul said, "Brethren, be not children in mind: yet in malice be ye babes, but in mind be men" (1 Corinthians 14:20). Don't hold a grudge. Yes, you will become angry at times and when you do you should express yourself, not hatefully, but honestly. Get it over with, and then forget it.

148

There was a story told about a man who drank heavily but was trying to quit. He would ask God to forgive him, but in a few days would slip again. Over and over he repented, and asked God's forgiveness. One day, after having slipped again, he prayed, "Oh, Lord, I've done it again." And the Lord said, "Done what?" The beauty of forgiving and forgetting! Develop this same quality.

*Be appreciative* of what your husband does for you, over and above his needful, everyday things. Let him know the joy you feel for his thoughtfulness. It could be that his taste in selection was not what you would have chosen. In fact, it might be atrocious. But had you thought that he went to the trouble of spending time and money in the selection of that gift, simply because he loved you? Learn to be truly appreciative, not only of the gift, but of his thoughtfulness and love.

3. Do not ask for things you know your husband cannot afford. He may try to get them for you, loving you as he does, when he could ill afford to do so. This may cause him to get in over his head, financially. Do not ask for his love, his affection, for gifts, or to be taken out more often. If you fulfill your role as a wife, these things will come as a natural by-product, thought of by him.

4. Retain your youthfulness as you grow older. Have a young outlook on life. Don't live in the past, but keep up with current events. I am not advocating that old people try to act like young people, for that is a most disgusting sight. But they should at least be able to "relate."

5. Don't withhold emotion. If you are happy, show it. If sad, do not be ashamed to cry. If you love a person, show them. This frank display of emotions makes for a more interesting person, one who is more natural.

6. Be self-confident. This trait has to be developed in most people, but it can be. Do not be an introvert. Get out of that shell. There are people who think everyone else can do things better than they can. There is only one thing worse; the person who thinks she can do everything better than anyone else. But if you are rather shy, and have this tendency to be an introvert, just remember this to help you: no one is as confident as he appears to be. Also remember

149

the world is not watching you nearly as much as you think it is. Work toward the goal of self-confidence by building an image of yourself by the way you want to be and then working toward fulfilling it.

7. Overcome that inferiority complex. This is closely akin to the one just mentioned. Sometimes people have this complex because of a lack of talents and accomplishments. This can be overcome. Learn how to do things well and work toward getting even better. Also remember that you can do something better than anyone else. No one is perfect in everything. All have their good points and their bad. Quit fretting about your lack of talents and get busy acquiring some skills. If it is lack of money and things that causes your inferiority complex, forget it. This is not important. Some of the best accepted and popular people I know have nothing in the way of this world's goods. Note the homes where kids like to congregate. The appeal is not because it is the largest and best equipped home. Education is another thing about which you should not feel inferior. Some of the most ignorant people I know are college graduates. People can be educated in many fields, and you can be self-educated in many things simply by doing. Be your own best teacher. Learn to do for yourself.

8. Learn to be a good conversationalist. Strangely enough, you do not have to do a great deal of talking to be considered a good conversationalist. It takes a good listening ear. If you are good at leading a person out, he will soon be doing all the talking. You will be surprised at how much he thinks of your ability to converse. Of course, you need to listen intelligently, and that requires some background material. So gather a store of knowledge. Read articles, watch news, acquaint yourself with what is going on in the world.

9. Retain your sense of humor. We haven't said much about this quality throughout this series of lessons, but I am convinced that a sense of humor is important. If you don't have a natural flair for humor, try to develop it. In situations that can begin to take on tragic undertones, a sense of humor can be your salvation. It can get you out of lots of difficult

150

and sticky positions. Most of all, learn to laugh at yourself. I know some very likeable people who tell funny and ridiculous stories *on themselves*. I think it a mark of bigness to be able to laugh at yourself, and especially at your own mistakes.

In conclusion, let us suggest that there are two sides to every person. In our study of the woman and her role, we should realize that there are also two sides to her. There is the spiritual, which emphasizes the qualities God has required of her in order to fill her role as wife and mother and homemaker. It requires her to be sober-minded and chaste, kind and in subjection to her husband.

The second side of woman is the purely physical. This side emphasizes and underscores the femininity she possesses; the happiness she radiates, and her childlike qualities. Of course these two work together to make one complete product, the woman we are, or at least the woman we hope to become.

We trust these practical suggestions will cause you to want to create the kind of woman God wants you to be. We trust we have been instrumental in creating within each one of you a desire to do a better job from henceforth than you have in the past.

We have learned that women sometimes need to be taught *how* to love their husbands. Are you a better wife now than you were when you began these studies?

There is no doubt but that you love your children devotedly, but hopefully you have come to appreciate what loving really means; giving your time, giving the child the spiritual training that will cause him to be a child of God, and to love him enough to discipline him when he needs it.

We trust the teaching we have given herein has caused you to think soberly about life, your responsibility as a wife and mother, and the awesome fact that you have a sobering job to do in this world; that you now recognize and live a chaste life, and are better equipped to teach the same things to *your* daughters.

Hopefully I have dignified the place of woman in your thinking when I designate her role as that of "keepers at home." I hope you think of this as the greatest of all roles woman can have, and that your place in subjection to your husband will cause you to find the fulfillment each woman so richly deserves.

Your study of these lessons is an indication to me that young women are greatly concerned about this topic. You are to be commended for wanting to know more about how to be a good wife and mother. If these things have been stressed and taught well enough to cause you to have more appreciation for your role, I feel the lessons have been worthwhile.

# Acknowledgements

In the preparation of these lessons I have relied heavily upon the counsel and advice of several. I owe a debt of gratitude to the following:

My husband, Floyd Thompson, who has stood by me, encouraged me in writing this work, and has been my best critic and counsellor. Without his help I would have floundered. After the preparation of each lesson he closely read and made necessary corrections. I am appreciative of his vast knowledge of God's word.

Brother Homer Hailey, who wrote the foreword for this publication, has been of inestimable help in the preparation of the lessons, and in the restructuring of sentences throughout. I am deeply grateful to him. Our friendship with him and his family has been one of the most abiding relationships of our lives.

Brother Brent Lewis, who has been of much help in finding help in the mechanics of printing, and other matters of this kind. This is a new field to me, and I am grateful for his knowledge of these matters.

The Bible has been my main source for this work, for without it we would have no basis at all for the things set forth herein. I have used the American Standard version throughout. Not only is my main outline taken directly from the Bible, Titus 2:3-5, but it is upon this inspired book that

I have relied for all the ideas set forth herein. In many instances modern society is violently opposed to the Bible. Throughout the work I have tried to point out that the Bible has guided mankind for centuries, and should continue to do so as long as time stands.

Other source books have been much help to me in outlining what I wanted to say. Some of these are: *Fascinating Womanhood* and *The Fascinating Girl,* both by Helen Andelin; *Woman, Her Blessings and Responsibilities,* by Irene Sowell Foy; *Counsel for Christian Youth,* by J. A. McNutt, Volumes I and II; *In the Hands of a Woman,* by Rachel Howard; and, *Martha, Martha,* by Marge Green.

I have tried to write my own work, relying on these sources only for ideas, rather than for "excerpts" or "word-for-word expressions." But many of my own ideas have been colored by what I have read, so that not always am I able to determine. I do not want to be guilty of plagiarism, and certainly it was not intentional if indeed it did occur.

CPSIA information can be obtained at www.ICGtesting.com
Printed in the USA
LVOW040718060113

314512LV00001B/3/A